MW00582611

Derashot LeDorot
A Commentary for the Ages
Leviticus

Norman Lamm

DERASHOT
LEDOROT
LEVITICUS

EDITED BY

Stuart W. Halpern

FOREWORD BY

Mark Dratch

The Michael Scharf Publication Trust
RIETS/YU Press
OU Press
Maggid Books

Derashot LeDorot
A Commentary for the Ages
Leviticus

First Edition, 2013

Maggid Books
An imprint of Koren Publishers Jerusalem Ltd.

POB 8531, New Milford, CT 06776-8531, USA
& POB 4044, Jerusalem 91040, Israel
www.korenpub.com

The Michael Scharf Publication Trust
of Yeshiva University Press

OU Press
An imprint of the Orthodox Union
11 Broadway
New York, NY 10004
www.oupress.org

The publication of this book was made possible through
the generous support of *Torah Education in Israel.*

ISBN 978 159 264 379 0, *hardcover*

A CIP catalogue record for this title is
available from the British Library

Printed and bound in the United States

Contents

Foreword   *xi*

Editor's Preface   *xv*

VAYIKRA

Chance or Providence?   3

Show and Tell   11

Sweet, Sour, or Salty? A Recipe for Religion   17

The Man in the Middle   23

TZAV

The Inside Story   33

SHEMINI

Moving Beyond Respect   43

Antiseptic Religion   47

As If Things Weren't Bad Enough   55

TAZRIA-METZORA

Aspects of Creativity 65
God, Man, and State 71
The Varieties of Vulgarity 77

AḤAREI MOT

The Normal Jew 87
Something Different for a Change 93

KEDOSHIM

The Meaning of Holiness 101
Let Criticism Be Welcome 107
How Relevant Should Halakha *Be?* 113
Out of Respect 121

EMOR

The Pursuit of Fun 131
The Kohen *Today* 137
So Help Me God 143

BEHAR

God or Mercury? 151
Our War on Poverty 155
Sons and Servants 161
In Praise of Impracticality 169

BEḤUKOTAI

Having the Capacity to Listen   *177*

The Tablets Within   *181*

In This Hour of Crisis   *189*

About the Author   *197*

About the Editor   *199*

Foreword

Mark Dratch

It is not for naught that the testimony of a relative – including that of a son-in-law – is invalid and, perhaps, tends a bit towards hyperbole. Nevertheless, this foreword, consisting of *devarim hayotzim min haleiv*, words that come from the heart, is a *milta de'avida leigluyei*, easily verifiable by all who know Rabbi Norman Lamm, who are challenged by his teachings, and who read his words.

God speaks. His first act is speech: "God said, 'Let there be light'" (Genesis 1:3). In fact, the entire creative process consisted merely of ten statements (*Avot* 5:1). God spoke to the patriarchs and to the prophets. God spoke at Mount Sinai and revealed not the Ten Commandments, but *aseret hadibrot*, the Ten Words.

And humans, created in God's image, are speaking creatures. Onkelos famously translates the biblical description of the creation of Adam as a "*nefesh ḥaya*" (Genesis 2:7), not as a "living soul," but, rather, "*ruaḥ memalela*," "a speaking spirit." It is this capacity of speech which distinguishes humans, known in the medieval lexicon as "*medaber*" (as opposed to mineral, vegetable, or animal), and it is this capacity of speech, which makes us most human, that is a function of the godly image in which we were created and makes us most divine.

I believe that Rabbi Lamm's words are divine – not in the prophetic sense, of course. They are inspired and inspiring. They are *ruaḥ memalela*, spirited and spiritual. They have their roots in a man whose brain is that of a Litvak, whose soul is that of a Hasid, whose DNA is that of a Galitzianer, whose disposition is that of a scholar, whose pen is that of a poet, whose eye is that of an artist, whose tongue is that of an orator, and whose heart is that of a *ba'al ḥessed*.

One of the many talents and gifts of Norman Lamm is his felicity with words, idioms, puns, and language. Through his pen, words are not merely tools of communication, but vehicles of inspiration and creativity. He luxuriates in their meanings, their nuances, their sounds, and their textures. In his sermons, Rabbi Lamm draws on his wealth of knowledge – he is well read in everything: Torah, Hasidut, literature, philosophy, science, history, and culture – and is able to communicate with a generation of Jews that is literate, cultured, engaged, and searching for meaning.

Sermons that are part of this and the other volumes of this series are the fruit of almost three decades of preaching. He is, as he called himself, an "unrepentant *darshan*" (see *Seventy Faces: Articles of Faith*, vol. 2, pp. 94-107). His natural talent for rhetoric and writing was nurtured by his father, Samuel Lamm, of blessed memory, who bribed him in order to encourage him to develop a vocabulary. His love and talent for *derush* was prodded by his uncle, Rabbi Yosef Baumol, of blessed memory, who gave him writing assignments on a regular basis and always demanded precision and style; by his teacher and mentor, the Rav, Rabbi Joseph Soloveitchik, of blessed memory; and by Rabbi Joseph H. Lookstein, of blessed memory, his teacher of homiletics at RIETS and first senior rabbi. But Rabbi Lamm ultimately succeeded because of diligence and hard work. He took sermons and language seriously. He sweated over the development of ideas and the crafting of phrases. And while he spoke only from a sketchy, abbreviation-filled outline paper-clipped neatly into the pages of his black Hertz *ḥumash*, he fully developed the sermon before Shabbat and then, immediately after *havdala* every Saturday night, sat at his typewriter to rewrite it and perfect it. The results are the hundreds of sermons on the Lamm Heritage website and the sermons that fill these volumes.

When I married Sara Lamm in 1982, these files filled the drawers of the cabinets of Rabbi Lamm's upstairs office. I confess that on many of our visits to my in-laws' Manhattan apartment, I would surreptitiously absent myself from the family and lock myself in the room – just the sermons and me. They transfixed me and transformed me. As a young rabbi, I had a personal treasure trove of the best *derush* and sermons – and they were all mine. (I must also confess how violated I felt when Rabbi Lamm donated these files to the YU library…now everyone had access to *my* stash!) I spent hours reading – no, listening – to his sermons, tasting the words, playing with his idioms, absorbing his style and trying it on for size. As did many of my colleagues who had access to some that had found their way to print in books like *The Royal Reach*, I even "borrowed" some of them. I learned quickly, however, that I could not deliver them effectively – they were uniquely his style, his voice. Nevertheless, they were model lessons to me for how to create great *derush* and how to construct dynamic, interesting, organized, profound, well thought out messages to which congregants just might pay attention.

Rabbi Lamm is a generous, demanding, yet forgiving teacher. In the early years of my rabbinate I would often discuss sermon ideas with him. He would prod me, challenge me, correct me. I sent to him my sermons in writing. They came back filled with the red ink of a meticulous, and often incredulous, editor. If I have any skill in writing today, I owe it to his prodding and critiques. When he and my mother-in-law visited, I would be more nervous delivering the sermon on that regular Shabbat morning than I would be in an overflowing shul on Rosh HaShana or Yom Kippur morning. But my in-laws, while constructively critical, were always gracious and unflinchingly supportive. For all of this – and for much, much more – I am eternally grateful.

In his sermon, "Words – Scarce and Sacred" (delivered *Parashat Ḥayyei Sara*, November 12, 1960 and printed in *Derashot LeDorot: Genesis*), Rabbi Lamm wrote,

> The more we use [words], the less they mean. When our rabbis investigated the first portion of Genesis, they discovered that the world was created "with ten 'words'" (*Avot* 5:1). Only ten words

to create an entire universe! And yet our rabbis were not satisfied. And so they asked, "Could not the world have been created with only one word?" Why waste nine precious words? Indeed, for with words, quantity is in inverse relationship to quality. If there are so many words that you cannot count them, then no individual word counts for very much.

Fortunately for us, Rabbi Lamm did not spare his words. Only one word, one sermon, just could not have done it. Rather, it is the aggregate of his many and varied insights that create an encyclopedia of faith, commitment, insight, and understanding. Like the Ba'al Shem Tov suggested regarding the primordial words of Creation – that they continue to echo to this day, sustaining and nurturing existence itself – Rabbi Lamm's many words resonate with new generations of readers who find inspiration in the aspirations of his sermons.

My in-laws, Norman and Mindy Lamm, raised children that are exceptional in many ways. I thank them for the gift that was their daughter, Sara, *zikhrona livrakha*, to whom I was married for thirty years and with whom I raised four incredible children until her recent untimely death, and with whom I shared love and unbounded laughter. She was my compass; she kept me grounded; with her, every day was full of surprises. Their grandchildren and great-grandchildren are exceptional as well, as are the children and grandchildren in-law. This is not the space to sing their praises. It is the space, however, to acknowledge the hard work and dedication of one grandson-in-law, Stu Halpern, who serves as the editor of this series. Stu is a phenomenon: loyal, dedicated, hardworking, committed, competent, and unstoppable. Even before one project ends, he begins three others. We are lucky to have him in our family (thanks, Ahuva and Erez) and so very proud.

Rabbi Mark Dratch is the Executive Vice President of the Rabbinical Council of America.

Editor's Preface

Stuart W. Halpern

I t is an honor to present to the reader this selection of Rabbi Norman Lamm's sermons on the book of Leviticus, from among the numerous *derashot* given by Rabbi Lamm between the years 1952 and 1976 in both Congregation Kodimoh in Springfield, Massachusetts, and the Jewish Center in New York, New York.

The book of Leviticus, dominated by the laws of the Tabernacle sacrifices, is an especially challenging book for a pulpit rabbi to draw from for the weekly sermon, and yet, in his addresses on Leviticus, Rabbi Lamm nonetheless captivated his congregants with his enlightening eloquence, drawing upon the book's eternal and relevant messages and values. Whether discussing the meaning of holiness, the contemporary role of the *kohen* (priest), or the relevancy of *Halakha* (Jewish law), Rabbi Lamm conveyed to his audiences that although the priestly sacrifices are no longer practiced today, the book of Leviticus still has much to say to modern man.

These sermons are presented as they were first articulated, with only minor editorial tweaks. The "current events" referenced in many of the *derashot* are an integral part of the power and relevance of the pieces, and thus those parts that describe them in detail have been

xv

retained so that the reader can best appreciate the historical and com-munal situation that Rabbi Lamm was responding to at the time. On occasion, the reader will note certain sensitivities of language that have developed since these words first were spoken.

Much gratitude is owed to the many individuals who assisted in the production of this volume. As these sermons were gleaned from the selection on the Lamm Heritage website at Yeshiva Univer-sity, many thanks go to the Dean of Libraries of Yeshiva University, Mrs. Pearl Berger, whose idea it was to create such a wonderful online collection of *derashot*. Many thanks to Ms. Hilda Tejada for her work in preparing this volume for publication, as well as to Kayla Avraham, Rabbi Yaakov Taubes, and Yigal Gross for their assistance. Rabbi Mark Dratch's helpful guidance throughout was truly invaluable, as is his moving and meaningful foreword. As always, this volume would not be possible without the enthusiastic encouragement from my wife, Ahuva Warburg Halpern, and the entire Lamm, Dratch, Halpern, and Warburg families. The publication of this book was made possible by the OU Press as well as the support of the Michael Scharf Publication Trust of RIETS/Yeshiva University Press, which, for many decades, has played a vital role in the production of Torah scholarship under the aus-pices of Yeshiva University.

From the moment they were first spoken, the words in this vol-ume cried out *"kitvuni ledorot,"* "write me for generations" (*Megilla* 7a). May they echo for generations to come.

Vayikra

Chance or Providence?[1]

Afundamental question, that has no doubt occurred to many of us here today, is: What is it that makes one person religious and another irreligious? True, there are obvious differences in practice: The religious person observes a special regimen of life, one directed by *mitzvot*, whether ritual or social or ethical, while the irreligious person does not observe this pattern of life. There are differences in commitments: The religious individual has faith and belief in one God, while the irreligious individual does not. But is there something beyond the formality of practice and the abstraction of faith, something more crucial to the basic outlook upon life that differentiates the believer from the non-believer?

I believe that this is the question the Rabbis proposed to answer in the incisive comments they gave us upon the first words of this morning's *sidra*, a word which also serves as the Hebrew title of the entire third book of Moses: *Vaykira*. In analyzing this one word, the Rabbis found looming before them two great historical figures, each pitted

---

1. April 2, 1960.

3

irrevocably against the other, two antonyms as it were. In the word "*vayikra*" itself they saw, of course, the figure of Moses. Our verse (Leviticus 1:1) reads: "*Vayikra el Moshe,*" "And He [God] called to Moses." If you eliminate the last letter of the word "*vayikra,*" you remain with the Hebrew word "*vayikar,*" "And He met, chanced upon, happened upon." The second word raises the image of the pagan prophet Balaam, for about him is it written later in the Bible (Numbers 23:4), "*vayikar Elokim el Bilam,*" "And God was met by Balaam." So the difference occasioned by this one letter shows the difference of two attitudes to God, one by Moses and one by Balaam. Moses hears the "call" of God; Balaam just happens to meet Him casually.

Our Rabbis (Leviticus Rabba 1:13) sharpened this difference and explained it thus: Concerning the "call" to Moses, "*vayikra*" is meant to connote "*leshon ḥiba, leshon zeiruz, leshon shemalakhei hasharet mishtamshim bo,*" "the language of love, of inspiration or activization, the language used by the ministering angels"; whereas concerning the attitude of Balaam, "*vayikar*" – the casual meeting with God – connotes "*leshon arai, leshon genai, leshon tuma,*" "the language of casualness and temporariness, the language of shame and disgrace, the language of uncleanliness."

This then is what our Rabbis meant in answer to the question we raised. One of the fundamental differences between the religious and the irreligious personalities, one of the major factors that makes one person devout and another skeptical, is the approach and the attitude to the significant events of life. If you look upon these major events of your life as mere chance, just luck or happenstance, as "*vayikar,*" an either lucky or unlucky accident – then that is the mark of an essentially irreligious person, that is the mark of *tuma*: unclean, irreligious. But if you look upon the events of life as being ordered occurrences, decreed by the supreme intelligence of God, and under His conscious direction, as providence rather than as chance – then that is the indication of a religious personality, that is the spiritual language of a religious person, the language of *malakhei hasharet*, ministering angels. So whether we see life as chance or as providence, as "*vayikar*" or "*vayikra,*" depends upon and also determines whether we are religious in outlook or not, whether we speak the language of *malakhei hasharet* or *tuma*.

And Balaam and Moses are distinct archetypes. Balaam, the man of *"vayikar"* and *tuma,* encounters God, but acts as if he had merely stubbed his toe against an unseen rock, shakes himself off, and goes on his merry way – unchanged, uninspired, passive, with an attitude of *arai.* Moses, however, the man of *"vayikra"* and *malakhei hasharet,* undergoes the same experience as did Balaam – the meeting with God – but he conceives of it not as a mere accident, but as a call, as a challenge flung to him from the heavens, as a summons to action, as an opportunity for *zeiruz* and *ḥiba.*

A Balaam-type personality would have celebrated Passover as merely a Jewish July 4th. He would have called it *Ḥag Yetziat Mitzrayim* – the Holiday of the Exodus – or *Ḥag HaḤerut* – the Holiday of Freedom. He would have celebrated what he regarded essentially as a merely fortuitous configuration of natural, political, and diplomatic events. The whole of the Exodus he would have interpreted as a merely lucky accident and celebrated his good luck. A Moses, however, and the people of Moses, those who understand the language of *malakhei hasharet,* would have preferred to call this holiday by the name of *Ḥag HaPesaḥ* and *Ḥag HaMatzot.* "Passover" means that God passed over the Jewish homes and struck only the Egyptians – this was not a matter of chance, but a deliberate, conscious act by God Himself. We refer to it as the Holiday of the *Matzot,* indicating that the Israelites put their faith in the prediction of Moses and the promise of God. The Exodus was not a matter of chance; it was divine providence. How we look, therefore, upon this greatest of all historical events in the life of our people is determined by an attitude of *"vayikra"* or an attitude of *"vayikar."*

But in addition to this choice of *"vayikra"* or an attitude of *"vayikar,"* of chance or providence, proving to be the basic distinction between a religious outlook and an irreligious outlook, between an attitude of *tuma* or an attitude of *malakhei hasharet,* there are practical consequences in our own lives as well. Besides being a measure of religion or irreligion, the attitude to life as chance or as providence also will determine, ultimately, whether or not in the entire panorama of life we shall learn to take advantage of opportunities or let them slip by us. Our Rabbis meant for us to understand this when they referred to the distinction between these two attitudes as, on the one hand, the language of *zeiruz* – inspiration or activization – or, on the other hand, the language of *arai*, casualness and impermanence. The man of "*vayikra*," the Moses type, the one who views life as a revelation of providence, will be one who has the capacity for *zeiruz*: he will view all of life as a divinely given opportunity for self-development and service. He will view the great events of existence as a challenge to which he must respond, a call to which he must answer. All of life becomes an active inspiring series of opportunities which can be seized and developed. The person of "*vayikar*," however, the Balaam type, he who views all of existence and all of life as merely chance and accident, for all of life will remain *arai* – just luck, bad or good, good fortune or misfortune, events never directed to him nor meant for him, and hence no necessity for answer or response. The great events of life will just slip by him – he will never view them as opportunities and therefore never take advantage of them. What to a Moses is a personal call is to a Balaam an impersonal, casual accident.

Moses sees the burning bush. Had he been a Balaam he would have regarded it as an improbable confluence of temperature, pressure, and oxygen, conditions resulting in the appearance of a flame without the bush being consumed. But he was Moses, and so he saw the revelation of providence. He therefore took the opportunity, seized it, and rose to this great destiny as the father of all prophets. In our *sidra* he hears the call of God – and gives Israel the opportunity to worship in its own way. Balaam, on the other hand, only chances upon God. He hears no call to which he feels compelled to respond. And so, from a meeting with God he ends up with a friendship with a Balak, the pagan king. He hears the voice of an angel – and ends up in a conversation with a mule.

Moses, who sees all of life as providence, sees two Jews fighting – and uses the opportunity to teach them the love of fellow man. He sees an Egyptian fighting with a Jew – for Moses this is the opportunity to put into practice his concept of social justice. He sees the shepherd persecuting the daughters of Jethro – this is a personal call, a challenge to take the opportunity to help the oppressed. That is how he becomes *Moshe Rabbenu* – teacher of Israel and the world.

With Balaam, the man who sees all of life as casual chance, it is completely different. The same opportunities are given to him – but he does not recognize them as such. Balaam was, according to our Rabbis, a counselor in the court of Pharaoh. He could have done something about liberating the Hebrew slaves. He did not.

He was hired by Balak to curse the Jews. It was an opportunity for Balaam to straighten out his primitive companion. He did not.

Balaam had the ear of the ancient pagan world. He could have taught them something about real, true religion. He did not. That is why Balaam, the man of chance, never grows, never develops. He dies ignominiously – murdered and despised.

No wonder that the ancient Jewish custom is that a child who begins his or her study of the Torah begins not – as we do today – with Genesis, the chronological beginning, but rather with the third book, the book of *Vayikra*. It is as if the entire cumulative Jewish tradition told the youngster now beginning his or her study of Torah: At this time that you are beginning your career as a Jew, remember that there are two attitudes to life. The attitude you must take is that of "*vayikra*" – you must view all of life as a great call by God to you personally. You must accept everything in life as a direct challenge given to you by heaven, as a divine gift of opportunity for you to seize, to develop, to grow with, in order to contribute all that you have and you are to the betterment of Israel and mankind.

Finally, in addition to the distinction between chance and providence providing a clue to religiousness and whether or not a man will make use of opportunities, it provides us with a major distinction as to whether life is worth living, as to whether our existence is meaningful, as to whether human happiness is at all possible. This is what our Rabbis meant by making the further distinction between *ḥiba* (love, warmth) and *genai* (shame and disgrace).

For the man of "*vayikra*," he who views life as providence, life does have the possibility of *ḥiba*. Even if life is sometimes painful, even if often it seems that most of it is a prolonged agony – still life can be lovely, it can be meaningful. I may not know why I am being subjected to pain, but if I recognize that God does know, that although I do not know its meaning at least God knows its meaning – as Job learned in his day – then that is a source of consolation for me. It means that my suffering is not devoid of meaning. Life still retains its inner worth. Life still is *ḥiba*.

If, however, my attitude is one of "*vayikar*," that it is all a matter of chance, then all of life is *genai* – a horrible, cruel, meaningless joke. If that is my attitude to life, then even if mostly good and happy events happen to me, my existence can have no real, lasting value. Even if – as with Balaam – I should meet up with God Himself, still all of life can be an existence that is *genai*, meaningless and worthless. What for the man of "*vayikra*" is a meaningful emergence from darkness into light, an adventure in growth and development, is for the man of "*vayikar*" nothing of the sort. For him life is just a dimly lit hallway in which man stumbles meaninglessly, beginning from the great black void of prenatal obscurity and ending in the limitless abyss of emptiness and nothingness with which life comes to an end.

How interesting that so many modern people, who often attain riches and health and luxury, are yet profoundly miserable. For having lost contact with God, they view all of life only as chance and accident. For them life is *genai*, a shameful void. While at the same time, a deeply religious individual, even if he does not have this wealth and health and luxury, can attain happiness. For that person knows that life has meaning, and therefore, for that individual, it has *ḥiba*, love and warmth.

How great, then, is this distinction between our outlooks upon life. The difference between "*vayikra*" and "*vayikar*" is truly amazing. And as if to accentuate the magnitude of the seemingly little difference between attitudes, the Jewish tradition declared that the last letter of the word "*vayikra*," the letter *alef*, be an *alef tzeira* – an *alef* written smaller than usual. There is only very little difference, the Jewish tradition meant to tell us, between "*vayikra*" and "*vayikar*." And yet the consequences are almost infinite.

Indeed, these consequences must loom before us at every moment of our lives. The Harvard historian Oscar Handlin, in a book treating eight crucial events in American history, speaks of the zigzags of history as "a line made up of a succession of points, with every point a turning point." Any moment in our lives and in our Jewish history is also a turning point. And it is only that little *alef*, that seemingly tiny distinction between "*vayikra*" and "*vayikar*," which will make all the difference in the world. At this turning point in our lives, we can either let life turn at will, subject to blind chance – "*vayikar*" – or accept it as a personal challenge and opportunity – "*vayikra*."

If "*vayikar*," then history is only a meaningless zigzag. If "*vayikra*" – it is a glorious upward curve in which man fashions his own destiny in a rising gesture to his Maker.

If "*vayikar*," then man sits back like an outside spectator, sardonically smiling at the curious unfolding of events he is powerless to influence. But if "*vayikra*," then he remembers what the Torah says at the end of the creation of the universe (Genesis 2:3): "*asher bara Elokim la'asot*," "that God had created to make" – that to God, Creation is only a beginning which man must develop, make, and create further.

If "*vayikar*," then the world is governed by cruel blindness of chance, and the Greeks were right when they referred to it as "Fortune." But if "*vayikra*" – then Israel was right, and all of life and history is merely the manifestation of *yad Hashem*, the hand of God, about which we can rightly say "*beyadkha afkid ruḥi*," "in Your hand, we commend our spirit" (Psalms 31:6).

If "*vayikar*," then Shakespeare, in *Macbeth*, was right, and life is only "a tale told by an idiot, full of sound and fury, signifying nothing." But if "*vayikra*," then Rabbi Akiva was right, and "*haviv adam shenivra betzelem*," "lovely and happy is man that he was created in the image of God" (*Avot* 3:14), and his life therefore is filled and pregnant with meaning and worthiness.

To all of us here, today and every day, God calls: "*vayikra*." May we indeed learn to view life as the call of God. May we learn to accept and make use of the opportunities He gives. May we learn to accept life as meaningful and worthy, so that for all of us life may become "*leshon ḥiba, leshon zeiruz, leshon shemalakhei hasharet mishtamshim bo.*"

Show and Tell[1]

Oone of the offenses for which the Torah, in this morning's *sidra*, declares the sin offering obligatory is that of *shevuat ha'edut*, that is, one who is under oath to testify and fails to do so. If a man witnessed some significant matter, either seeing or knowing of some facts important to some other individual who asks him to testify, then, "*im lo yagid*," if he withholds his testimony and refuses to testify, "*venasa avono*," "he shall bear the burden of sin" (5:1).

To those many amongst us whose first reaction, upon witnessing an accident, is to escape the scene quickly so as not to be bothered by innumerable court appearances, the Torah addresses its reminder that offering up truthful testimony on behalf of another person is not only a legal obligation, but also a religious and ethical one. There are three types, the Talmud tells us (*Pesaḥim* 113b), whom God despises, and one of them is he who withholds testimony needed by another. The truth is destroyed not only by outright falsehood, but also by failing to report the true facts.

---

1. March 30, 1963.

In a larger sense, the sin of "*im lo yagid*" refers not only to a trial currently in session in some courtroom, but to keeping your peace and remaining silent in the face of obvious injustice. To withhold testimony means to suppress your righteous indignation when by all standards of decency it should be expressed, and expressed vigorously. For even if there is no human court willing to hear the facts and correct an unjust situation, there is a Heavenly Judge before whom we are required to testify. He, therefore, who suppresses the truth and chooses silence in the presence of evil, shows his contempt for God, who is the King who "loves righteousness and justice" (Psalms 33:5). To a generation which lived through the Hitler era, and saw millions of Germans remain submissively silent while six million Jews were butchered, we need not stress the teaching of today's *sidra* that "*im lo yagid*," if one fails to cry out and bear witness, then "*venasa avono*," that individual bears guilt and sin.

Need we look far for sufficiently compelling examples against which simple decency requires us to declare our protest? There is the perennial problem of man's cruelty to man – and on scales both large and small. In all these cases, "*im lo yagid*," if we fail to testify to our deeply held conviction that mankind is created in the image of God and hence sacred, we share in the guilt.

For instance: In the past year there were two cases, one of them only this past week, in which a prize-fighter was pummeled to death in front of large audiences who paid handsome prices to be permitted to be spectators to this act of athletic homicide. Is it not about time that our country civilized itself and outlawed this public barbarism? Is it not stretching the point, to say the least, when the governor of this state defends this "sport" by calling it a "manly art"? Is it not a deep source of embarrassment to our country that the prize fighter who dealt the death blow came to this country from Cuba, given that in that country, ruled by tyrants and infested by Communists, boxing is outlawed?

Or more importantly: The Israeli government brought to the attention of the world this week the shocking news of West German scientists working in Cairo on developing "unconventional" weapons, including nuclear missiles. Dare the world keep silent and refrain from testifying to the sordid story of what German scientists once did to the

Jewish people? The West German government recently showed, in the *Der Spiegel* case,[2] that it can act decisively where its interests are concerned. It must do no less now. "*Im lo yagid*" – if the Western countries, ours included, suppress their protests, then "*venasa avono*," they shall compound the guilt of two decades ago.

Most especially does this principle of "*im lo yagid*" apply to the Jew. Our very reason for being Jews is to testify to the glory of the Creator. Our essential function as the people of Torah is to bear witness to the truth of Torah in word and deed. In the words of Isaiah (43:21) at the beginning of today's *haftara*, "I have created for Myself this people so that they might relay my praises"; or, with even greater cogency, the famous words later in the same *haftara*, "*ve'atem eidai*," "and you are My witnesses" (44:8). That means that every Jew must ever be self-conscious, must realize that we represent Torah, that everything that we do and say is an *eidut*, a testimony offered up on behalf of God and Torah. If a Jew acts shamefully, he disgraces his faith. If that individual acts meritoriously, that person brings credit upon Torah and its Giver. "*Im lo yagid*" – the Jew who, no matter how honorable his intentions, does not act with the dignity and respectability of a *ben Torah*, who fails to bear witness to the glory of Torah, "*venasa avono*," bears the guilt of having failed the most important mission in life. To the Jew, all of life must be – to use the name of the schoolchildren's game – "show and tell," an opportunity to show by example and tell by words that Torah civilizes man and raises him to unprecedented heights of nobility.

Parents of young children, those who have the opportunity of seeing most directly the effect and influence of one generation upon another, know well the secret of *eidut*. Children are not nearly as impressed by expression as they are by example; they emulate rather than obey. Only if a parent bears living testimony to his convictions will it be meaningful to a child. That is why it is of no avail to send a child to shul or school. You must *bring* the child to shul and school. Otherwise,

---

2. An article in the October 8, 1962 issue of *Der Spiegel* magazine described the sorry state of Germany's armed forces, and in response the magazine was accused of treason and its offices were raided by the police.

the child may go through yeshiva, but the yeshiva will not go through the child. "*Im lo yagid*" – if parents do not, in practice, live the kind of lives they want their children to lead, then "*venasa avono,*" the children bear the burden of their parents' guilt.

Rabbi Samson Raphael Hirsch has maintained that the word "*eid,*" "witness," is related to the word "*ode,*" "yet" or "still." To testify means to continue, to keep alive, to make permanent. To be the *eidim* for God means to keep alive faith in Him, to make the Torah ethic permanent, to continue the Jewish tradition into the future.

It is for this reason that we Orthodox Jews in particular ought to be so very concerned not only by the impression we make upon outsiders, but also how we appear to our fellow Jews who have become estranged from our sacred tradition. We have labored long and hard and diligently to secure an image of Orthodox Judaism which does not do violence to Western standards of culture and modernity. But at times the image becomes frayed, and another, less attractive identity is revealed. All too often of late we have been careless and coarse. Sometimes we have made it appear that we are barely emerging from the cocoon of medievalism. If we are to be witnesses to Torah, then Orthodox Jews must have a more impressive means of communicating with non-observant segments of our people. Saadia Gaon pointed out a thousand years ago that the best way to make a heretic, an *apikores,* is to present an argument for Judaism that is ludicrous and unbecoming. Orthodoxy cannot afford to have sloppy newspapers, second-rate schools, noisy synagogues, or unaesthetic and repelling services. When you testify for God and for Torah, every word must be counted – and polished!

It is highly significant, in this connection, that the Torah groups two other sins together with the one of "*im lo yagid*" as requiring one type of sacrifice for atonement. The other two, in addition to the sin of withholding testimony, are *tumat hamikdash vekadashav,* that of defiling the Sanctuary or other holy objects when we are in a state of impurity as a result of contact with a dead body, and *shevu'at bituy,* the violation of an oath. What is the relation between these three?

There is, I believe, an inner connection that is of tremendous significance. The person who violates "*im lo yagid,*" who suppresses the truth, especially one who fails to proclaim by example and expression the greatness of Torah and Torah life, is, as it were, acting as if all that individual believed in and all that individual represents were a corpse – a dead body of uninspired doctrines, irrelevant laws, and meaningless observances. The committed Jew, who, by acting cheaply or meanly, withholds testimony to the holiness of Torah, acts as if Torah were a dead letter insofar as it has no influence on character and conduct. By concealing this testimony that person has introduced an element of *tuma*, of deadly impurity, into the community. Furthermore, that person has also violated his *shevua*, for every Jew, by virtue of being born Jewish, is under prior oath to represent God, to stand for the Torah He gave at Sinai. We were commissioned to be a *"segula,"* a "treasure" of God (Deuteronomy 7:6), by being a *"mamlekhet kohanim,"* a "kingdom of priests" (Exodus 19:6), and that means, according to the Seforno, that we must directly and indirectly teach the entire world to call upon God and be faithful unto Him. Any Jew, therefore, who acts disgracefully, unethically, or irreligiously, misrepresents his mission, and violates his sacred oath.

It is for this reason that the *Halakha* was concerned not only with inner realities but also with outer appearances. A breakdown in our functioning as *eidim* means the introduction of *tuma* and the violation of *shevua*. It is for this reason, too, that the *Halakha* establishes a special and more taxing code of behavior upon the *talmid hakham*, the scholar – and, we may add, what is true for the scholar amongst laypeople is equally true for the observant or Orthodox Jew among the non-observant. That is why a Jew strongly identified with Torah must not accumulate bills but pay them at once; must not associate with unworthy people; must not be loud and abusive; must be respectful and courteous; must be scrupulously fair and ethical in business; and must be beloved and respected by all. When a Jew, especially a Torah Jew, or any Jew connected with a synagogue and especially an Orthodox synagogue, acts in conformity with this kind of code, that individual bears witness to the loftiness of Torah, to its divine origin, and demonstrates that Torah is a living reality, not a corpse which emanates *tuma*; that individual keeps the millennial oath, administered at Sinai, by which God is represented to the world. No wonder Maimonides, in codifying the special laws of which we have mentioned several examples, places them in his Laws of the Foundations of the Torah – for indeed, these are fundamental to the whole outlook of Torah.

Perhaps all that we have been saying is most succinctly summarized in two letters in the Torah. In the words *"shema Yisrael,* hear O Israel, *Hashem Elokeinu,* the Lord is our God, *Hashem eḥad,* the Lord is One" (Deuteronomy 6:4), the *ayin* of *"shema"* and the *dalet* of *"eḥad"* are written in the Torah larger than usual. These two letters spell *"eid"* – witness. For indeed, just as *"im lo yagid venasa avono,"* suppressing this testimony on behalf of Torah is sinful, so if we are *eidim,* and do testify to Him by our lives – that is the greatest tribute to the One God, Lord of Israel, and Creator of heaven and earth.

Sweet, Sour, or Salty? A Recipe for Religion[1]

Judaism counsels moderation and rejects extremism. This teaching of moderation in character is raised by Maimonides to a fundamental principle of the *Halakha* and is elaborately described by him in the first part of his immortal Code of Jewish Law, the *Mishneh Torah*.

Furthermore, this "Golden Mean" of abjuring the extremes and choosing the middle of the road in conduct is identified by Maimonides as nothing less than the "*derekh Hashem*," "the way of the Lord." This is what the Torah means, according to Maimonides, when before the destruction of Sodom the Lord says (Genesis 18:17): "Shall I hide from Abraham what I am doing? For I know him that he will command his children and his household after him that they shall observe the *derekh Hashem* (the way of the Lord), to do righteousness and justice." While Sodom veered to the extremes, Abraham walked in the "way of the Lord," doing justice and righteousness, following the Golden Mean. This is what is meant by the "heritage of Abraham," the priceless possession of our people.

---

1. March 25, 1966.

According to this "way of the Lord," one should develop the kind of character that is distinguished neither by anger and temperamental tantrums nor apathy and indifference; he should be neither a spend-thrift who squanders every dollar, nor a miser who cannot bring himself to spend a cent; he must be neither giddy nor gloomy, neither in a state of manic joy nor in a state of somber depression. One must always try to keep one's mood and one's quality of conduct moderate, stable, and thoughtful. Of course, there are exceptions, and Maimonides describes them in detail. But the general principle remains: Keep away from all extremes in conduct.

This fundamental of Jewish ethics was discovered by a renowned rabbi in, of all places, today's *sidra* on the laws of the sacrifices. Rabbi Joseph Saul Nathanson, the eminent halakhic decisor who was Rabbi of Lwow, thus interprets symbolically the commandment concerning the *minḥa*, the meal-offering on the altar (Leviticus 2:11), "No meal-offering, which ye shall bring unto the Lord, shall be made with leaven; for ye shall make no leaven (*se'or*), nor any honey (*devash*), smoke as an offering (*taktiru*) made by fire unto the Lord." Rabbi Joseph Saul points out that leaven, or sourdough, and honey, represent two extremes of taste: sour and sweet. Neither is permissible on the divine altar. The two extremes of sour and sweet symbolize the extremes of human character, and therefore are rejected. If life is conceived of as a *minḥa laHashem*, as a gift offered to God, and if life is to be lived as *ketoret*, as incense, as harmonious and pleasant, then it must be neither *se'or* nor *devash*, neither sourdough nor sweet honey. The laws of sacrifices thus offer us a symbolic hint of the Golden Mean.

Yet there is a danger that people will overstate the theory of moderation and reduce it to an absurdity. They might conclude that one must always choose the middle of the road. Hence, if you are faced with the extremes of, on the one hand, *kashrut*, and, on the other, those who are non-kosher, then one might interpret the Golden Mean to rec-ommend being only half-kosher, or to have a kosher home but to be non-kosher outside the home. One might reduce it to the ridiculous conclusion that if some feast on Yom Kippur and some fast, then one should simply eat lightly or just skip breakfast, in an effort to be mod-erate. It might mean that if some are Orthodox and some are Reform, then the teaching of moderation urges that everyone be Conservative; or that between the extremes of truth and falsehood, one should always tell a half-truth!

Is this, indeed, the *"derekh Hashem,"* "the way of the Lord?" Obviously not! In fact, it is Maimonides who, in the introduction to the *Guide for the Perplexed*, tells us that if he has a very difficult passage to teach, and he can teach it to one wise man only at the risk of displeasing ten thousand fools, then he prefers to address his remarks to the one wise man and take no note whatsoever of the multitude of fools. Surely this is not the seeking of a mathematical average as an application of the principle of moderation!

What then does it mean to be moderate? What are its limits? I believe the answer is this: In matters of character and personality, in developing the traits wherewith one reacts to the world, in teaching oneself personal habits, there must be only the Golden Mean and one must keep a healthy distance from extremes. But when it comes to principle, to ideals and philosophy and commitments, to a code rather than a mode of conduct – then only the vision of truth may guide us. And truth is radical; sometimes it will lead us to a middle position, more often to one extreme or the other. Let us remember that, as the Rabbis (Deuteronomy Rabba 1:10) pointed out, the Hebrew word for "truth" is *emet*, and these three Hebrew letters allude to a symbolic truth. The first of these letters is the first letter of the Hebrew alphabet; the second letter of *emet* is the middle letter of the alphabet; and the last of the three letters is the last of the Hebrew alphabet. In other words, truth may be found at either extreme or right in the middle – there is no predicting in advance where it will lead us. In my faith and in my practice of my principles, I must follow only the truth. There is no conflict between moderation in character and truth of ideals. A person may be liberal or conservative in his views; that is a matter of that individual's principles. In that person's expression of these principles, however, he ought to be moderate. But the principles themselves are beyond any rule of moderation. Whosoever tries to live his life and work out his destiny merely by finding the middle point equidistant from the extremes, and squatting there, surrenders his critical judgment and yields to a disgraceful, dull, deadly, depressing conformism, which can only kill one's character. Here, only truth must be our guide. To travel automatically in the middle of the road is to exercise neither intelligence nor humanity. The renowned Kotzker Rebbe, reflecting on the traffic condition of his society, said that only *beheimot*, animals, walk in the middle of the road – not human beings. We, reflecting the traffic conditions of our own society, might say that the middle of the road is the most dangerous place of all – one can be hit from both sides.

Certainly, if you find yourself in a society of extremes, where some are promiscuous and some highly moral, some honest and some deceitful, some believe in God and some are virulent atheists – Judaism's teaching of the Golden Mean does not mean to say to you: be half moral, tell half a truth, believe in half a God. You must, of course, be utterly moral, totally truthful, and completely devout – even if that condemns you as an extremist and marks you as off-beat. Therefore, in questions of *Halakha*, a decision may sometimes be extreme; that does not matter, for our only guide is *emet*, truth.

Does this mean, however, that in dealing with principles, such as *Halakha*, that since I may go to an extreme, therefore my expression of it may be uncivil and even reckless? Certainly not! Here is where character is required. For even people with extreme views must express them moderately. In articulating the truth, in living by it, I must always consider others – their conditions and their sensitivities. My opinion may be unpopular, but my presentation of it ought to be non-repulsive.

Perhaps this is the essence of what was meant by the great prophet Malachi, who, in describing the ideal man, the perfect *kohen*, uttered the immortal phrase (2:6): "The law of truth (*emet*) was in his mouth, and no unrighteousness was found on his lips." What the prophet meant to say about the ideal priest was that in his mouth, internally, in his own vision of his ultimate commitments, there was only the "Torah of truth" – no other consideration may be entertained. But when it came to expressing this truth to his fellow human beings, to bringing forth his vision from his mouth, within, to the words that appeared on his lips, without, then while he never changed this vision, he did not allow it to be expressed with unrighteousness, with ugliness, with contempt for others. The greatness of the *kohen* described by the prophet is that his ideals are uncompromising, and yet the character of his expression is so very attractive.

Perhaps this is what the Torah meant when, in prohibiting *se'or* and *devash*, sourdough and honey, symbols of the extremes in conduct, it added affirmatively that "to every sacrifice that is offered up on the altar, thou shalt season with salt" (Leviticus 2:13). What does this mean? In character there must be no extremes, neither sweet nor sour. Ideals must always follow the vision of *emet*, of truth. But even then, even when we follow truth without compromise, we must keep it flavored, we must season it with a bit of salt. We must see to it that the truth we serve up is neither bland nor harsh. Salt, unlike sweet or sour additives, is not essentially a flavor added from without; rather, it enhances the flavor inherent in the food itself, it brings out the best within it. So too, the salt of the sacrifice is a symbol of the attitude we must bring to Torah – it reveals the inner beauty of Torah itself.

Permit me to give you some examples. The *Halakha*, as the Torah of truth, may sometimes decide "forbidden," and sometimes "permitted." This is the *emet*, the truth, and should be acknowledged as such. Nevertheless, the decision of *Halakha* must always be applied with a pinch of salt. For instance, even when the Torah says "forbidden" and we are required to communicate this prohibition to our fellow Jews – we must rebuke our friend who does wrong (Leviticus 19:17) – nevertheless, there remain limiting principles, such as when we know that our rebuke will not be accepted, it is better not to offer it in the first place, so that the fellow Jew who violates the commandments will do so unwittingly and out of ignorance, rather than out of spite and willfulness (*Beitza* 30a). Similarly, the *Halakha* may sometimes say: yes, such and such is permitted; nevertheless, do not put this permission into practice (*Shabbat* 12b)! Often the *Halakha* will urge a man to refrain from a technical permission on the grounds that one ought to sanctify himself by accepting self-restraint even where the *Halakha* is essentially permissive (*Yevamot* 20a).

At other times (*Pesaḥim* 83b) we are told not to practice what is permissible in front of others who do not regard this particular act as being permissible. Such conduct is dictated by the "salt" in our religious diet. The correct recipe for religion, therefore, is: "neither sweet nor sour, but salty."

These thoughts are of utmost significance especially this Sabbath when, from the pulpit of this synagogue, as well as several neighboring synagogues, we shall read to you a special announcement concerning the construction of an *eruv* in Manhattan. This *eruv* permits carrying in the island of Manhattan under certain conditions and with certain restrictions. Within those limits, it is an unqualified halakhic decision, very long in the making. Without question, one may henceforth carry in Manhattan with the exceptions, as noted, of such items as are considered *muktza*.

Nevertheless, in actual practice, we urgently recommend "salt." Although the truth is that carrying is permitted, we ought to add sacrificial salt by practicing some self-sacrifice in exercising common sense, discretion, and good taste. Do not overuse the *eruv*. Make only minimum use of it. Do not exploit it. Please refrain from all obvious and open violation of what others may, in good conscience, still regard as wrong.

The recipe for religion requires, in this case, as in every other case, tasteful discretion and proper understanding that will contribute to both the holiness of the Sabbath and the enjoyment of the Sabbath.

May God grant that our actions be acceptable before Almighty God as both *ketoret* and *minḥa*, as a gift of our spiritual endeavors, and as a pleasant and harmonious contribution to the welfare of all Israel. Amen.

The Man in the Middle[1]

The key verse in our *sidra*, which introduces the entire subject of sacrifices, reads: "*adam ki yakriv mikem korban laHashem*," "When any man of you bringeth an offering unto the Lord" (Leviticus 1:2). The Zohar, intrigued by the use of the term "*adam*," declares that by this word, "man," the Torah means neither the first man nor the last man. Rather, the Torah is concerned with the faith, the devotion, and the love of all mankind in between man at the very beginning of time and man at the very end of time.

What the Zohar tells us is that for the first man and the last man, devotion to the Almighty is not an extraordinary achievement. The first man, Adam, lived in Paradise, he had every indication of God's bounty, and his communication with the Lord was clear and direct. Certainly, it required no great moral effort for him to believe in and worship God. Man at the end of time is one who will have experienced the complete redemption, and who will have enjoyed the divine revelation at the termination of history. For him, too, faith will not be an act of moral

---

1. March 18, 1967.

heroism, for he will have seen the hand of God acting in history. For these individuals, paradoxically, *korban* is not a sacrifice, and loyalty to the Creator is not a particularly noteworthy *mitzva*. But it is for the man in the middle of the course of history, for the Adam who flourishes neither at the beginning nor at the end of time, for whom *korban* is a sublime accomplishment. For man in the middle of the course of history, for whom certainties are elusive, for whom faith is so difficult, who dwells neither in Paradise nor in a state of redemption – for him *korban* and *emuna* are an unexampled and unparalleled triumph of the human spirit (see *Ateret Mordechai* by Rabbi Mordechai Rogov).

The real *mitzva* is accomplished when the *korban laHashem* is offered by man who finds himself in the middle of time and history, his horizons beclouded by uncertainty, his heart filled with fear, his innards pulled apart by anxiety, and his prayers doomed to frustration.

The period we live in is such a middle period, neither at the beginning of time nor at the end of time. We live in a time that the Bible has called *hester panim*, the hiding of God's face, when we yearn for some experience of His presence, but we are disappointed; when we strive to communicate with Him, but receive no answer; when we are willing to submit our very lives to him, but we fear that He doesn't care; when He seems to have vanished from our midst without leaving a trace; when life appears meaningless and existence absurd. How easy for modern man, living in the middle of this *hester panim*, to yield to despair, to cease praying, to quit believing. And it is precisely because of this that it becomes his crowning achievement to believe despite doubt, to hope despite despair, to continue to pray despite divine silence. It is this high resolve of the "man in the middle" performing the act of faith that makes him a true *adam*, a true human being.

But I believe that the verse we have just discussed and interpreted is meant as more than a compliment to the "the man in the middle" who retains his faith, and more than an encouragement to continue on his way. I believe that if we examine this verse carefully we shall also find in it the beginnings of an answer to the question of questions for modern man, the man in the middle: How and where shall we discover the sources of faith? How shall we acquire *emuna sheleima*, complete faith, in a world gripped by skepticism, in a society soaked in cynicism, in a civilization that has permitted holocausts and obscenities known as concentration camps? How shall we be *adam* in an age which is neither first nor last? How shall we offer ourselves up *laHashem* when we dwell neither in Paradise nor in a state of complete redemption? How shall we emerge from bedeviling doubt into the fortitude of faith? What advice do we have for that man in the middle who would like to believe but finds that he cannot?

I believe we can find three suggestions that await us in our verse. Let us take them in the order in which they appear.

First, "*adam ki yakriv*," if a man "*yakriv*" – that word means not only to offer up, but also to draw close, to come *karov*, close, to God. Faith is not a gift that magically appears out of heaven and graces the lucky individual. It is something which requires great and strenuous effort. *Emuna* is not a state; it is a process which demands study and experience and thinking and willingness and labor and diligence.

In Judaism, unlike other religions, we do not accept uncritically the apparently logical idea that faith must precede religious practice. On the contrary, Judaism prefers the psychological truth to the logical statement, and holds that *emuna* and *mitzva* feed on each other, that often leading the right kind of life will bring man to the right kind of belief. It is possible for a man to believe – and yet to live like a pagan. However, if man will live like a Jew, even if he thinks like a pagan, ultimately he will come to think and believe as a Jew should, too.

In the Jerusalem Talmud (*Ḥagiga* 1:3), the Rabbis put, as it were, into the mouth of God some very bold words: "*halevai oti azavu ve'et Torati shamaru*," "Would that the Jews abandoned Me as long as they observed My Torah!" That is, let the Jew hold in abeyance his belief in God, as long as he studies Torah, performs *mitzvot*, and leads a moral and ethical Jewish existence. For then, having experienced Judaism pragmatically, he will ultimately arrive at *emuna*: "*hase'or sheba haya mekarvan etzli*," the inner leavening agent of Jewish existence will bring him back to God. In other words, "*adam ki yakriv*" means that man must take the initiative in reaching out to God; he must commit himself to Jewish living, in the confidence – which Judaism promises us will be vindicated – that this kind of life and these kinds of deeds will lead him to become *karov*, close, to Almighty God.

Now this refers not only to a commitment of deeds, but also to a commitment of emotions. I recommend that you read, if you have not already done so, Elie Wiesel's *Jews of Silence*, his description of his visit to Russian Jewry. He describes the current generations of Russian Jews, young people who were never permitted to hear a Jewish word, to learn a Biblical verse, to hear a single tale or law of the Talmud. Their minds were filled with nothing but materialism and Marxism, and they consider themselves good Russian Marxists. Yet, they also prefer to be known as Jews, no matter what the risk. And how do they express this nascent and latent love of Judaism and the Jewish people? What is it that brings them back to the synagogue? Not the *shofar* on Rosh HaShana, not even *Kol Nidre* or *Ne'ila* on Yom Kippur, but the singing and the dancing on Simḥat Torah! We, in America, all too often take these festivities on this holiday in a sense of amusement, as a semi-humorous manifestation of levity. Yet in Moscow, every fall, on this day, in front of the Great Synagogue, thousands of young Jewish Marxists gather together to sing and to dance their devotion to Judaism! "*Adam ki yakriv*" – these are Jews, long alienated by the strong hand of Communism, who are drawing close by committing their emotions, by committing their joy and their happiness, to Judaism! No matter what they believe intellectually, no matter how they live the rest of the year, this commitment of their deepest and their most cherished emotions of Jewish joy is an indication that there survives in them the "*pintelle yid*," that precious dot of Jewishness that, with the help of God, will someday bring them completely back to Judaism and, it is our fervent hope, to the State of Israel.

The first means of rediscovering the sources of faith, then, is to live as a Jew, both in general conduct and in emotional attachments, and thereby return to full Jewish faith.

The second means is by remembering that faith, in Judaism, is not entirely personal and individual; it also reflects the experience of our whole people and its history. That is why we speak of ourselves not as individuals who, all together, constitute a people, but rather as individuated members of *keneset Yisrael*, the congregation of Israel. That is why prayer is encouraged by individuals in their homes, but it is preferable that we worship in a *minyan*. The faith that each individual Jew has or seeks can be strengthened by associating with other faithful Jews, so that all together we will find strength in each other.

Thus, the next word of our key verse is: "*mikem*," "from amongst you" – "*adam ki yakriv mikem*." We can become the right kind of spiritual *adam* only if we issue from the right kind of *mikem*, only if we seek our most intimate associations with people who have similar inspirations and aspirations. That is why our Rabbis commented (*Ḥulin* 5a) on "*mikem – velo mumar*," that this excludes the willful heretic, that in our Sanctuary we may not accept the sacrificial offering of one who rejects God with malice aforethought.

We have spoken often of the need for modern Orthodox Jews to view their fellow Jews, with whom they disagree and from whose opinions they dissent, with love and understanding, and that in general we must open ourselves up to the modern world and the best of its culture. But that does not mean that we must break down all the defenses that life and nature permit us; that we must yield our most intimate lives to the pervasive non-Jewish influence of the great world around us. It means that we must seek out for our own closest friendships those who will serve to enhance our religious devotion rather than to detract from it. It means that we must create for ourselves the right sort of family environment, that we must seek the proper communal milieu, and live only in an appropriate residential area where we can enjoy the kind of society that will help us in our aspirations to find Jewish fulfillment in life. Only one who is possessed of foolhardy self-confidence can believe that he can survive with his Jewishness intact in a neighborhood or society where Jewishness is either ignored or derided; and such a person stands condemned of committing spiritual suicide. We must know in advance that we will not remain Jewish if we move into a literally God-forsaken neighborhood just because we prefer the social status of certain exclusive areas. So too, we can have little hope for our children to remain in the Jewish fold if we send them to schools in remote areas in which Jewishness is an oddity, and if we let them spend their summer vacations in children's camps where the word "Torah" is never heard.

The third means to full Jewish loyalty I find in the next two words, "*korban laHashem*," "an offering to the Lord." I base this idea on a discourse by one of the greatest teachers of *Mussar* in the last generation, Rabbi Eliyahu Dessler of England and Israel (see *Mikhtav MeEliyahu*, vol. I, pp. 32-39). We all know that mankind is by nature acquisitive.

Psychology teaches it, experience confirms it, and we know it intuitively. From the moment a person is born he begins to grasp whatever he can. What we do not sufficiently appreciate, however, is that there is another and opposite tendency that is indigenous to human beings: the desire to give as well as to receive. That humans should possess this wish to give is, from the Jewish point of view, only natural. For our tradition teaches us that mankind is created in the image of God, which means that in many respects we resemble the Creator. And God has no need to take from us; He only gives. That is why one of His attributes is *ḥessed*, love, or the capacity for giving of Himself. The very creation of the world, as King David puts it in Psalms (89:3), is an act of *ḥessed*, "*olam ḥessed yibaneh*", and the revelation of Torah is an act of giving and *ḥessed* as well. Therefore man, created in His image, resembles the Creator in possessing this inherent desire to give of himself.

Connected with this concept of giving is the fact of love. It is worth pondering, says Rabbi Dessler, which comes first, or which is cause and which is effect – the act of giving or the act of love? Does a person love first and then give to his beloved because he loves, or is it perhaps reversed – that an individual gives and as a result that individual loves? That we normally bestow gifts upon those we love – that is fairly evident. What is less evident, but equally true, is that the act of giving itself enhances love and often creates it. When I give of my time and my substance and my talents to another human being, I feel I have invested in him or in her and therefore my attachment and my affection and love grow every time I give and in proportion to what I give. In this sense, the giving is the cause and the loving is the effect. The Rabbis taught us this same truth: "If you desire to love your friend, do something good for him!" (*Derekh Eretz Zuta*, ch. 2).

This advice is most pertinent for young couples about to be married – or even married already. Whatever you do, do not make demands upon each other! It is the quickest way to frustrate the development of true conjugal love. This is one time that an Orthodox rabbi pleads with his people not to live according to the *Shulḥan Arukh*! It is a sad state of affairs when a couple must adjudicate their differences by reference to the code of Jewish law. The *Shulḥan Arukh* elaborates the claims of a husband upon a wife and a wife upon a husband. And when a couple is reduced to legal action based upon mutual claims, they are in desperate trouble indeed. The ideal of Jewish married life is to live so that there shall be no need to resort to the arbitration of Jewish law. Therefore, there should be no demands upon each other – instead, each partner must make it his or her business to give and give and give. It is the only way to transform infatuation into love, momentary attraction into permanent bonds – give your time, give your loyalty, give your talent, give your affection, give pleasure and joy and happiness, give gifts, give attention and concern – and from this there will blossom love and ultimately the fruits of profound and lifelong affection and loyalty.

Now the same principle should be applied to religion. We have spoken of faith, but that is an abstraction. Jews prefer to speak of *ahava*, love, for that is about passion. More than believing in God, we are commanded to love Him. Judaism recognizes that the love for God is indigenous in the human heart; religion is not grafted on to us artificially from without, but pre-exists within us. The question is, how shall we express it and enhance it? And the answer is – "*korban laHashem*," you must learn to give to God. When we give of our time by getting up early to pray with a *minyan*, when we give of our substance to the causes of the Almighty, such as a synagogue or school or charity, when we give our attention and our concern to Him and His people, then the process of giving enhances the love we bear for Him within. The more we give, the more we love. The person who would like to believe but cannot, ought to learn how to give – then that individual will not only believe, but will also love.

In summary then, how does one become an *adam* in this middle of time? First, one must commit, in action and emotion, to seek out God. Second, one must provide one's self with a society and environment of Jewishness. And third, one must give of one's self and one's possessions to the Almighty and His causes, and then that individual will learn to have love, which is even more than faith.

When we have done this, we shall attain the status of *adam*, as genuine human beings in the middle of history. And then we shall deserve, in return, the attention and affection of the Creator. For the Midrash (Leviticus Rabba 2:8) tells us that the word *adam* has particular meaning; it is "*leshon ḥiba vileshon aḥva vileshon rei'ut*" – the language of divine love and brotherliness and friendship.

Tzav

The Inside Story[1]

Our Sages, who normally adhere strictly to principle and are unconcerned with popular reactions and public opinion, show a remarkable divergence from this method in a comment that has relevance to this morning's Torah reading. The end of our *sidra* tells us about the *milu'im*, the consecration of the priests for their service in the Temple. In addition to the various ceremonies that had to be performed, the priests were commanded "and from the door of the Tent of Meeting ye shall not go out for seven days" (Leviticus 8:33). For a full week they were required to stay within the "Tent of Meeting," that miniature Sanctuary which was later to become the institution of the Temple. The Talmud (*Yoma* 2b) derives there from other laws as well, among them that the High Priest had to remain within the Temple for seven days before Yom Kippur. Every year he was to set aside this week and remain completely within the Sanctuary, in a chamber known as the *lishkat parhedrin*, to prepare himself for the holiest day of the year.

---

1. March 20, 1965.

Now, as we all know, any room or house which serves as a residence requires that we affix a *mezuza* to the doorpost. Nevertheless, for certain reasons, the Temple rooms were exempt from this obligation of *mezuza*. Hence, the *lishkat parhedrin* did not require a *mezuza*. However, Rabbi Judah (*Yoma* 10b) is of a somewhat different opinion. He maintains, together with his colleagues, that no chamber of the many chambers within the Temple required a *mezuza*. The *lishkat parhedrin*, the chamber where the High Priest stayed for seven days, similarly did not require the *mezuza* insofar as the law was technically and officially concerned. However, Rabbi Judah maintains that the Rabbis promulgated a special decree requiring only of the *lishkat parhedrin* that it be adorned with a *mezuza*. The reason offered by Rabbi Judah for the Rabbis' decree is amazing: "so that the people will not say, 'the High Priest is imprisoned in the Sanctuary!'" Rabbi Judah said that the Rabbis feared that when the people congregated during the High Holy Days around the Temple, they would notice that after the High Priest went into the Sanctuary until after Yom Kippur he did not emerge for seven full days. Not noticing a *mezuza* on the doorpost, and therefore not considering the *lishkat parhedrin* as his personal residence, they might be led to the fantastic conclusion that as a result of some inner court politics the High Priest was incarcerated in the Sanctuary! Therefore, in order to avoid such a public misinterpretation, let there be a *mezuza* affixed to the doorpost on the *lishkat parhedrin*, so that the people will consider this chamber as the High Priest's residence and not regard him as a prisoner within the Temple walls. This decree, according to Rabbi Judah, was made, as we moderns would be wont to say, to safeguard the "image" of the priesthood.

More remarkable than this rare example of the concern for the opinion of the unlearned masses is the vast difference between the real facts and the distorted impressions. Here was the High Priest, the cynosure of all eyes, the focus of the attention of all Israel as they gathered in Jerusalem on the holy days, representing his people before his Creator in Heaven, engaged in spiritual exercises of the highest order, reaching the very zenith of his career in this marvelous consecration of his whole personality to the great spiritual tasks that lay ahead of him on Yom Kippur – what greater joy, what more poignant delight? Yet an uninstructed public that cannot emancipate itself from its petty and prosaic prejudices comes to the bizarre conclusion: The High Priest is imprisoned in the Sanctuary! They do not see the High Priest engaged in the normal insignificant details of their own trivial lives, no going in and no going out, no rushing to work and no coffee breaks, no entertainment and no luxuries, and so they assume that the High Priest is locked up within. Were it not for that *mezuza* on the doorpost of his chamber, the public indeed might consider the High Priest imprisoned!

How does such a jarring discrepancy come about, that people can consider a man in jail when he is at the heights of his joy, that they behold a burden when he experiences a blessing? The answer, it would seem, depends on how you view the Sanctuary of Judaism – as an insider or as an outsider. If you look at the Sanctuary from the point of view of an insider, you gain a totally different view from that of an outsider. If you are an outsider looking in, a spectator, you can never experience that which the insider does: the subtle joys, the daily delights, the sense of newness and rebirth. Viewed from without, the priests appear as prisoners, when in fact they are princes of the Lord! From without, all one can see is the High Priest incarcerated; whereas the High Priest as the insider experiences the feeling of being – as the Torah puts it – "*lifnei Hashem*," "before the Lord" – a rare opportunity for an ennobling and elevating awareness of God's ineffable Presence. But this is something that an outsider cannot know any more than – to borrow and modify a parable from the Ba'al Shem Tov – one who looks into a room from the street, beyond sound-proof windows. He does not see the musicians who stand on the side, and he does not hear the music; he sees only people dancing. Inside, the dancers hear the music, and they respond with the joyous rhythm of their whole bodies. But he, the outsider, sees only meaningless gesticulations, and what appear to him as the weird convulsions of the demented.

This tendency to be an outsider is a fact of life in general today. Social thinkers from psychologists and sociologists to philosophers comment regularly about the phenomenon of "alienation." It affects every aspect of thought and activity of contemporary man. A recent philosophic conference, well reported in the press, came to this conclusion: Today we know more than ever before – but we understand less. We have become statistic dilettantes who peddle figures but are alien to life's profoundest experiences; who can quote prices and fact and costs and numbers, but who have failed to take the plunge into life's bittersweet mysteries.

And how eccentric and distorted is the view of the perpetual outsider! For instance, one who does not sense the historic drama of the struggle for human equality and dignity in our days may view the Northern civil rights enthusiasts who travel to Selma to demonstrate as publicity-seekers or, at best, unfortunate young people who have foolishly traded in the conveniences of home for the discomfort and danger of a civil rights demonstration. Such a skeptic is completely oblivious to the thrill experienced by the insider, that joy of participation in a great human cause that penetrates to the marrow of the bone. Similarly, outsiders find it hard to understand why American Jews are so agitated about the lack of *matzot* for Russian Jewry, about the fact that 300,000 Jews in Kiev will this year have no *matza*. They fail to appreciate that this is more than merely a secular-democratic protest for the freedom of religion; were it but that, we would have many other things to object to, and not only concerning the oppression of Judaism. But *matza*, as an insider appreciates, is the awareness of being linked in the historical chain that goes back to antiquity; it is, as well, the symbol of fellowship with other Jews in the present, even those beyond the Iron Curtain; and it is the hope that just as once before Israel experienced *yetzi'at Mitzrayim*, so will it someday experience another *yetzi'at Mitzrayim* – this time, the exodus from Russia, and from all other houses of slavery in modern days.

Indeed, when it comes to religion, especially Judaism, this difference between those within the Temple and Torah and those without it becomes more pronounced. More than once do I recall from my own experience being introduced to a well-meaning stranger as an Orthodox Jew, or rabbinical student, or Orthodox Rabbi. To my infinite annoyance there spreads on the face of the stranger the look of incredulousness, and he says: "Orthodox – and you are so young!" As if Torah were an affliction brought on by old age, a kind of spiritual geriatrics. How frustrating and often how futile to have to explain that to be "frum" is not to be a fossil and to be religious is not to be a relic. How amusing and yet how tragic to have to explain that we observe Torah not because we are imprisoned in the Sanctuary, not because parents force us or circumstances coerce us or because of habit or fear or need, but because we love and desire to live a meaningful Jewish life *"lifnei Hashem,"* "before the Lord."

No doubt many of those here today have had similar experiences. Someone learns you are an observant Orthodox Jew, and he clucks his tongue in sympathy, feeling genuinely sorry for you, and responds in a half-admiring and half-pitying tone: "You observe the Sabbath, with all its restrictions? You cannot smoke or travel or write?" And we must explain: Sabbath is for us not a day of gloom and restriction, but one of *oneg*, unadulterated joy, when (without being an ecstatic mystic) an ordinary observant Jew can experience a *neshama yeteira*, the "additional soul" that comes from a day of pure rest and re-creation, when we feel liberated from the tyranny of all the pettiness that surrounds us during the week. Or someone discovers that you believe in and practice the laws of family purity. And again the incredulous reaction, with a mixture of pity and admiration: "You really practice these ascetic regulations denying your basic drives?" And we have to explain so patiently: No, it is not asceticism, but a healthy and vital self-discipline, which ennobles the animal within us and purifies and sublimates it, and makes marriage a dream, not a nightmare. So we observe *kashrut* and we expect no awards and want no sympathy for it. It simply is part of our life of *kedusha*, the practical program of Jewish holiness and differentness. And the very fact of observance of *kashrut* away from home, with all the minor inconveniences it entails, by itself gives us the feeling of being at home everywhere!

Indeed in every area of life, the outsider sees only size and number rather than content and quality, the conventional rather than the moral, the fashionable rather than that which is indeed dignified, opinions rather than ideas. Such a person beholds a synagogue and can see only the membership and budget and activities and aesthetics. But that individual lacks that which the insider knows in the depths of his being: the heights of joy, the touch of mystery and grandeur, the whisper of the echo of the sound of the voice of God. No, we are not walled in the Sanctuary; we are welling up with hope, with courage.

For "*lifnei Hashem*," "before the Lord," means that in this society which suffers such solitude we do not experience that oppressive loneliness, for even if others abandon and neglect us, we know that God is with us. In this automated society with its tyranny of numbers and progressive depersonalization, this means that mankind, unlike so many of our new products, is not disposable and replaceable. It means that we have a function in the divine economy and a purpose of life. This indeed is the secret and reward of a genuine Jewish life!

Therefore, in order to avoid this fallacious and misleading conclusion about Jewish life, to prevent people from thinking that the pious Jew is a prisoner in a jail called Judaism, what must we do?

First, we must affix the *mezuza* on the *lishkat parhedrin*; that is, we must do all we can to inform those not heretofore exposed to Jewish life, the outsiders, of the particular quality of Jewish experiences. We must present it as dignified, decorous, and aesthetic.

Secondly, we who are insiders must reassure ourselves. A minority generally tends to adopt a view of itself held by the majority, the outsider. While occasionally this is a healthy practice and restores perspective, it must never become the standard way of self-definition. It is self-destructive always to view oneself through the eyes of others. I know too many observant Jews who always prefer to see themselves as others see us – from the secularist and Reform to outright assimilationist Jews, from the benevolent anti-Judaists to the vicious anti-Semites. When that happens, we begin to apologize for our beliefs, for our heritage, for our very selves; then we wallow in self-pity about the heavy burden that destiny has fated for us; then we begin to abandon real Judaism for what has been called "symbolic Judaism," with its few ceremonies for special events and an occasional synagogue attendance – but nothing more. So let us remember: no apologies and no self-pity! We are not captives in the Sanctuary of Judaism – we are its custodians. Torah is for us not a burden but a blessing.

Finally, while we are not missionaries, we ought to invite our fellow Jews who look in from without, to come in. A wine connoisseur does not judge the quality of a sample by the shape of the bottle or the print on the label or the personality of the salesman. There is only one test: Taste it! To look is not enough. So does the Psalmist declare:

"Taste and see that the Lord is good" (34:9). It is not enough just to see – one must also "taste." You cannot appreciate Judaism until you taste it and experience it and live *"lifnei Hashem,"* "before the Lord." Then it is unnecessary to be stimulated by artificial enticements, by the unnecessary *mezuza*, by the superficial prop.

"Blessed are those who come in the name of the Lord, seeking the Lord; we bless you from within the house of the Lord" (Psalms 118:26) – and invite you in!

Here, *lifnei Hashem*, before the Lord, you will discover that you are not in a prison, but in a palace full of pure spiritual pleasures and exquisite delights and the joy of life.

Taste and see – and you will discover "that the Lord is good" (Psalms 118:29).

Shemini

Moving Beyond Respect[1]

In today's portion we read of the tragedy that struck Aaron, the High Priest of Israel, when his two sons were devoured by a fire from the Lord when they ministered in the Temple and changed part of the regulations. We read that Aaron was silent at the time of this tragedy. Probably the grief, the inner protest, was too overwhelming for him to say anything at all. At this moment Moses turns to his mourning brother and says to him, "Through those who are close to me will I be sanctified (*ekadeish*), and before the entire people will I be honored (*ekaveid*)" (Leviticus 10:3). What is it that Moses told his brother, and that he wished to impart to all posterity, at this time?

There are two concepts that are mentioned by Moses: *kedusha*, holiness, and *kavod*, honor or respect. Both of these are worthy Jewish goals deserving of our highest aspirations. Yet, they are not equal to each other – one is a higher level than the other. *Kavod*, honor, refers to an attitude that is external to the soul. I honor or respect somebody, but that does not necessarily mean that I subscribe to his opinions. I admire

---

1.   March 23, 1957.

or give reverence to a great musician, although I may be absolutely flat and monotone. It is an external act of courtesy, a gesture that is sincere but does not involve my whole personality. *Kedusha*, holiness, contrariwise, implies an inner transformation, a total commitment and dedication of the entire personality toward the transcendent goal for which it strives. One can give *kavod* without being changed within. One cannot achieve *kedusha* until one has undergone a complete spiritual metamorphosis.

Now, *kavod* is something that the masses are capable of. *Kedusha* is something which only the initiates are capable of and obligated to achieve. Isaiah (6:3) proclaims even as we do thrice daily, "Holy holy holy is the Lord of Hosts, the world is full of his *kavod*." The Lord of Hosts, He who is above and beyond the world, is in His essence *kadosh*, holy. That is the highest realm and the highest level. But insofar as *kol ha'aretz*, the entire world, ordinary people, are concerned, all they can perceive is *kavod*, honor or respect.

Respect is a noble, good virtue. But it is antiseptic, it does not require the involvement of one's inner self. Sanctity, on the other hand, is a higher, deeper, profounder commitment. Therefore Moses said, "Before the entire people will I be honored," will I receive *kavod*. For ordinary people it is sufficient that they come into the Temple and minister, that they pray, that they observe the decorousness that is so appropriate in a House of God. For ordinary Jews, an attitude of *kavod* is about all that one can require of them. But when it comes to *kerovai*, those who are close to God, then *kavod* is not by any means sufficient; then only the transcendent and lofty goal of *kedusha*, holiness, is worthwhile.

This, indeed, is what Moses told his brother Aaron. You may in your heart of hearts feel aggrieved – after all, your sons were ministering to God in the Temple, their heart was in the right place; so what if they changed a part of the service? The answer is: An attitude of *kavod*, honor for God, is sufficient for ordinary people. For priests, for the children of Aaron, however, *kavod* is never enough. From them I expect a total dedication, the uncompromising commitment to *kedusha*, to holiness. If your sons failed, it is because as *kerovim*, those close to God, they have failed to aspire to higher *kedusha*.

This is part of our problem in American Jewish life today. We suffer from what Prof. Abraham Joshua Heschel has called "a theology of respect." People come into the synagogue and they respect it – therefore they need not learn from it. They respect Torah, they respect Judaism, they respect religious people, they respect rabbis. And therefore the whole thing is externalized, it never penetrates within their hearts and souls. What is required is a sense of *kerovai*, of being close to God and therefore setting up as our ideal goal not only *kavod* but *kedusha*. In recent years, with the so-called return to religion that we have witnessed, it has often seemed to me that as religion has become respectable, it has tended to become unholy; with its gain in prestige and external acceptance, it has lost some of its passion, its power of criticism, its totality, its involvement with mankind's most basic and fundamental destiny.

The *haftara* of this week indicates the same idea. We read of the Ark being taken captive by the Philistines and then being recaptured by David. David was overjoyed at the return of the Ark to the Camp of Israel: "and David danced with all his might" (II Samuel 6:14). His sense of joy and thrill was excited by this great event, and so he responded in a blazing passion of holiness, realizing in practice the words he was to write later in the Psalms, "All my bones say: 'Lord who is like unto thee?'" (Psalms 35:10). And then we read, in one verse "The Ark of the Lord was brought to the city of David" (II Samuel 6:16) – the great and wonderful moment when the holiness of the ages was stamped indelibly upon the city of Jerusalem – "and Michal the daughter of Saul watched from beyond the window." What a difference is revealed in the contrast between the attitude of David and that of his wife, the princess Michal! While David is involved with his people in the holy undertaking, she, the princess, heiress to the aristocratic traditions of her family, stands far and distant, remote and removed behind the pane of glass, watching her husband David involved with his people and with his joy and with his faith – "and she despised him in her heart" (II Samuel 6:16). She could not abide the whole theme of David dancing about the Ark. And so when her husband comes home to bless his home, she releases a torrent of abuse and reproach at him. How can you, she cries, dance there as though you were one of the commoners, with the maids and the servants and all the ordinary people? The whole corruptness of her attitude is revealed in two words in her first sarcastic barb at her husband: "*ma nikhbad*, what kind of honor, of respect, is it for the King of Israel to act the way you have?!"

This was the undoing of Michal the daughter of Saul. She was limited in her horizons. She could not see beyond the level of *kavod*. She was forever sealed off from a vision of *kedusha*. And therefore she did not understand that her husband had transcended the limits of *kavod* and had risen to the level of *kedusha*. No wonder that she was doomed to wither away and die and not leave any memory behind her.

This, then, must be our understanding, our duty and our ambition. It is important, of course, that our synagogues possess the element of *kavod* – of courtesy, of respect, of honor, of decorum. But it is far more important that they attain, as well, the ideals of *kedusha* – true devoutness, piety, and love of Torah.

When people come into a synagogue and listen to a sermon and they "enjoy" it – that is the level of *kavod*. When they are disturbed by it to the point of feeling they want to do something – then they are on their way to *kedusha*.

The rabbi who strives to institute decorum, respectability, and honor in his congregation, has made the steps towards *kavod* – an absolute prerequisite for a decent service. But that is not enough. The next step must be holiness, the establishment of a *kehilla kedosha*, a holy community. To be "inspired" by a synagogue, the services, and the sermon – that is *kavod*. To be moved by them to obey the message, to follow their line of thinking, to live the life of Torah – that is the beginning of the beginning of a life of *kedusha*, a life of holiness.

Antiseptic Religion[1]

We read this morning of the strange rite of the *para aduma*, the ashes of the red heifer which were used to purify one who had contracted levitical impurity by contact with a dead body, but which ceremony at the same time defiles the priest in charge of the act of purification. *Para aduma* has thus always been accepted as a mystery, a *ḥok* or incomprehensible law that defies reason in its paradoxicality. It is therefore an annual reminder that important as reason is in the life of religion, it is not the totality of religion. If mankind understood all that religion and God demand of it, it would not need divine revelation; indeed, mankind would displace God as the center of life, and all authentic religion would thus come to an end.

Para aduma therefore tells us that intelligent as human beings are, and as much as they must endeavor at all times to exercise their intelligence, their intellect nonetheless remains limited. God, as Creator and Source of all intelligence, transcends mankind's intellect. Life conceived

---

1. April 1, 1967. This *derasha* addresses the subject matter of *Parashat Para*, the extra Torah portion often read on the same *Shabbat* as *Parashat Shemini*.

47

only in terms of reason or logic is shallow. It is even monstrous, like a person with an oversized head and an undersized heart.

The idea that pure reason is a sufficient guide for an individual through life is sophomoric, and it is an index of intellectual adolescence. One might even describe it with that worst of modern epithets – it is non-modern, medieval. Modern science emerged only when it denied the omnipotence of reason, when it cut itself off from the tyranny of pure reason. Natural science does not at all come to its conclusion on the basis of logic, but on the basis of empirical evidence – testing, experimenting, investigating. Indeed, one of the greatest theories of modern physics, concerning the nature of light, embodies a logical contradiction – it violates the principal of reason that a thing cannot be two opposites at the same time.

This does not mean to say that science affirms faith and religion. It does mean that shallow rationalism is a thing of the past. Rashi (Numbers 19:2) tells us that the *para aduma* was a source of vexation for Jews in their confrontations with the non-Jewish world – the nations of the world would taunt and deride the Jews because of the apparently unreasonable nature of *para aduma*. Today, such taunting sounds silly indeed.

However, we must be prepared for the challenge in response to such an assertion – "Is this not an instance of blind faith?" Most Orthodox Jews, rabbis or laypeople, have had to put up with such reproach at one time or another, when trying to explain that we observe even if we do not understand the reason for every observance. What do we answer to this charge of "blind faith?"

First, let us always remember that such pejorative and emotion-laden terms always confuse, rarely clarify. Who is to say which faith is blind and which not? Usually, one person's blind faith is another's fearless determination; what I believe is far-sighted vision, and what the other one believes is silly superstition.

Of course, faith can be blind – but it also can be luminous and enlightening and insightful. The *emuna*, faith, that transcends reason, as symbolized by the *para aduma*, is founded on a sense of confidence in the divine intellect, on trust that God, in His infinite wisdom, knows what I in my limitations can never know. Thus, the first time I send a child away from home, I do so on a basis that is usually irrelevant to reason. Is this blind faith – or is it confidence? When I submit to a medical doctor for a very serious and delicate operation, though I know almost nothing about the technicalities of surgery and medicine – is this blind faith or confidence? It is blind faith only if I only project my own wishes irrespective of the objective situation. It is confidence if I use a wise intuition, an overview which integrates all the nuances of the situation, and hence is more than merely the facts and reason. "Who is the wise man? One who sees the consequences that will be born from the present situation," our Rabbis taught (*Tamid* 32a). A computer cannot do this; only a wise person can.

Certainly, then, mankind does not live by reason alone, even though reason helps to make order and sense out of life's experiences. Love, hate, fear, ambition, sentiment, friendship, passion, desire, suffering – these are not matters of reason, yet they are the stuff of real life. Similarly, human beings possess a religious dimension to their personalities, one that cannot be reduced merely to reason or to psychology. This is what Rabbi Shneur Zalman, founder of Habad Hasidism, called "*ahava tivit umesuteret*" (*Tanya*, ch. 44), the natural but concealed love for God that inheres in a person, and what the great German-Jewish thinker, Isaac Breuer, referred to as "*hatzad hahazoni*," the prophetic dimension of human personality (see his *Tziyunei Derekh*). And *para aduma* reminds us that this religious or spiritual or prophetic dimension is not subservient to reason or any other aspect of personality; it is separate, independent, and autonomous as a feature of human life. Without it, we deny mankind its very humanity and reduce it to nothing more than a biological computer. And religion as such, if it is based only on reason, becomes antiseptic and lacking in drama and depth. Furthermore, it is the kind of religion that cannot really survive a crisis. The great author of the *Or HaHayyim* (Yosef Yavetz, d. 1505) has told us, from his personal experience, that when Spanish Jewry was expelled in the fifteenth century, those Jews who observed the Torah and the *mitzvot* out of faith alone, the simple Jews, were able to demonstrate remarkable heroism and prefer exile and banishment to baptism, whereas the sophisticated Jews, who prided themselves on their knowledge of philosophy and their use of "pure reason" instead of "blind faith," were the first ones to submit to Christian pressure to kiss the cross.

But if so, we face a direct and troubling challenge: Does this mean that reason has no role in Judaism? Obviously it does have a role. Furthermore, what of the Jewish rationalists, such as Saadia Gaon and Maimonides? Did they not insist that Judaism not only can but should make use of *sekhel*, reason? In fact, the saintly Rabbi Bachya maintained that if a man has the capacity to use reason and philosophy in his religious thinking and does not do so, he commits a sin in the eyes of Torah (*Ḥovot HaLevavot* 1:10). How shall we fit this emphasis on reason into the context of a Judaism which proclaims a law of *para aduma*, which speaks of the importance of *ḥok*, which declares the autonomy of *emuna*?

The answer is that no Jewish thinker ever believed that people can fully understand God and Torah by reason alone, without any assistance from revelation. *Para aduma* is the corrective for this, giving us the capacity for intellectual embarrassment, teaching us intellectual modesty. Hasidim used to say that that is why a man should cover his head. Clothing is worn for one of two reasons: either to keep one warm or because of modesty. Our heads are covered not because we fear the climate, but because it is an act of modesty – we cover the cranium to show that no matter how brilliant we are, our intellect nevertheless remains sorely limited before Him, the God of infinite wisdom. *Para aduma* similarly teaches us this kind of modesty and prevents us from indulging in intellectual arrogance.

But if we cannot reach God by reason alone, why did the great Sages of Israel in the Middle Ages devise the classical proofs for God's existence? These proofs, truth to tell, were not potent enough to convince the agnostics, and they were essentially unnecessary for one who already believed – as did these same Sages of Israel. Why then did they offer them? Why did they emphasize the role of reason?

The answer that I wish to commend to your attention is one that touches the very foundations of Judaism itself. It is an insight provided to us by one of the foremost disciples of the late Rav Kook, Rabbi Yaakov Moshe Charlop. He teaches us that people have many dimensions to their personalities, among them: emotion, actions, ethical bent, and intellect.

Our sacred duty is to reveal God's presence, to make Him manifest, to bring Him into this world on every level and every manner. Mankind's purpose is *legalot et hanistar*, to take the potentialities for being aware of God – potentialities and possibilities which inhere in every atom of matter and in every moment of life and in every aspect of personality – and actualize them, expose them, reveal them, bring God to our awareness and to the consciousness of every human being. That is why we must use all dimensions of life to reach Him. We ought to experience Him with our emotions. We ought to act practically so as to build the *malkhut shamayim*, the Kingdom of Heaven, actualizing the will of God for mankind and its society; and so too we must understand Him rationally and therefore demonstrate His existence through the use of intellect and philosophy. None of these alone is sufficient; all of them together constitute the human paean of praise to the God of all perfection.

This is what the *para aduma* does for us – by telling us that there is something beyond our reason, it challenges us to reach God by all means, by exercising every aspect and fiber of human personality. It does not deny the value of reason at all, but it tells us that it is not enough to feel Jewish, or to think Jewishly, or to act Jewishly; rather, we must do all three – and even more. It reminds us that the human personality is infinitely rich and multifaceted, and all of it must rise in one great spiraling symphony of devotion to God. "*Kol atzmotai tomarna*" (Psalms 35:10) – "all my bones," each and every aspect of my life and my energy and my time and my personality, must proclaim, "Who is like You, O Lord?"

The great Rabbi of Kotzk once said:

> "*Frum iz shlecht*" – to be pious is sometimes to be cruel, for a man of piety is subject to the weakness of self-righteousness which results in insensitivity to the feelings of others.
>
> "*Gutz iz ni'uf*" – excessive goodness and generosity can lead to immorality, for in my goodness I may try to satisfy the whims and passions of another without regard to moral restraint.
>
> And, "*Klug iz krum*" – to be bright is often to be crooked, for brilliance frequently degenerates to mere shrewdness or craftiness.

Any of these virtues by itself can prove exceedingly damaging. However, he added, "*Uber frum un gut un klug – dos iz a Yid!*" "But to be pious and good and bright – that constitutes a Jew!" No one aspect of personality should be overdeveloped at the expense of any other – all together must rise to the Creator of the world.

Para aduma is thus not a doctrine of the denial of reason, not a proposition basing faith on absurdity. It appears now in a new meaning, teaching us the inadequacy of any single explanation of mankind, any single mode of life, any single way of reaching the Almighty. *Para aduma* confirms human beings' marvelous complexity, it affirms the mystery of our personalities – it assures us of a religion which is not flat and antiseptic but varied and colorful and deep and comprehensive and even mysterious. It tells us that humans and God meet on many levels, indeed on all levels. Therefore, no person is ever cut off from God because he was born inadequate in any one aspect of his personality. Some people may be impoverished in their intellect, some in their emotions, some in their ability to practically implement the divine design for the world; but everyone has some opportunity to reach out to Heaven.

It has been asked: Should not our special portion of this morning begin with the words "*zot ḥukat hapara*," "this is the law of the *para aduma*," even as we read elsewhere "*zot ḥukat hapasaḥ*," "this is the law of Passover" (Exodus 12:43)? Why does our portion begin with the word "*zot ḥukat haTorah*," this is the *ḥok*, the law, of all the Torah? I suggest that this is the beauty of Torah itself, that it includes preeminently *ḥok*, the integrating element, the principle that no one aspect of life or character is sufficient, but that all aspects together are required and demanded of us.

A Jew is not a disembodied intellect who does nothing but philosophize; not an ecstatic and ascetic, nor a monastic mystic; not one who believes, and believes that his belief alone will bring salvation; not an obsessive observer of ritual or ethics who does what he does without feeling or understanding. None of these alone is enough – we need all, and even more than all of these. "*Zot ḥukat haTorah*" – when we have a Torah, we have the principle of *ḥok*, along with *ḥokhma* and *ma'ase* and *regesh*, reason and action and emotion.

And when we have these, we have then achieved wholeness as well as holiness, for both holiness and wholeness are the goal of Torah. "*Torat Hashem temima*," "The Torah of the Lord is whole" (Psalms 19:8) – it is perfect and comprehensive. And through our study and observance of Torah we can achieve this wholeness and thus we will discover that Torah is also "*meshivat nafesh*," it restores wholeness to the human soul and personality.

Having understood and experienced this, we shall then learn to appreciate the next verse: "*pikudei Hashem yesharim, mesamḥei leiv*," the laws of the Lord are straight, they are meant for the ultimate benefit of mankind even if we do not understand them at the present, and they make the heart – and the mind and the soul and society – glad and happy.

As If Things Weren't Bad Enough[1]

Our *sidra* begins by describing events in the Tabernacle on the first day when it actually was used for the service; or, if we include the seven days of the consecration of the priests, the eighth day. "*Vayehi bayom hashemini*," "And it was on the eighth day" (Leviticus 9:1).

The Rabbis (*Megilla* 10b) were extravagant in describing the significance of that day: "That day [when the priests first began their ministrations] was an occasion of such great joy before the Holy One that it was equal to His joy on the day that heaven and earth were created." The textual reason for this equivalence between the day of Creation and the day of ministry at the Tabernacle is the similarity of expressions in the two verses of, "And it was on the eighth day" and (with regard to Creation) "And it was evening and it was morning, the first day" (Genesis 1:5).

Now, while we may have some kind of textual excuse for drawing this analogy, the question yet remains what the Rabbis really meant by comparing the first day of the Tabernacle to the day of Creation.

---

1. April 8, 1972.

One of our commentaries offers an answer that is full of insight and of the greatest importance to us. He refers to the midrash (Genesis Rabba 19:7) which states that God originally intended that His *Shekhina* (Presence) dwell here on earth. However, when mankind sins, God's *Shekhina* rises to increasingly higher heavens. Thus, the midrash continues to describe how when Adam sinned, the *Shekhina* left the earth and ascended to the first heaven. When Cain killed his brother, the *Shekhina* rose to the second heaven. In the generation of Enosh, the *Shekhina* was banished to the third heaven; in the generation of the Flood, to the fourth; in the generation of the Tower, to the fifth. The events of Sodom caused the *Shekhina* to ascend to the sixth heaven. And finally, the persecution in Egypt banished the *Shekhina* to the seventh, or the highest of the heavens. In order to rectify this situation, seven righteous people arose, one in each generation, and they acted so as to bring the *Shekhina* back down to earth. These seven were Abraham, Isaac, Jacob, Levy, Kehat, Amram, and Moses.

Hence, the purpose of Creation was that God's presence, His *Shekhina*, dwell on earth. That is why the first day of Creation is such a source of joy to the Holy One. On the day that the service began in the Tabernacle, the Divine Presence was also manifest on earth, and therefore He was as happy on this day as on the day He first created the world.

What the Sages mean to tell us in all this is not a detailed geography of the heavens. What they are doing, I submit, is offering us a new definition of the key Jewish concepts of *kiddush Hashem* and *hillul Hashem*, of the sanctification and desecration of the divine Name. To sanctify God's Name means to bring Him closer to mankind. To desecrate His Name is to create a distance between God and mankind, to make Torah appear remote, forbidding, irrelevant, impertinent. When one acts or speaks so that Judaism appears far off and of no direct concern to living beings, such a person has desecrated the divine Name.

I have chosen this theme not only because of the text, but also as pretext. I am troubled by the forbidding, remote, and hostile image Orthodox Judaism has developed in American and international life. Unfortunately, this week *The New York Times* carried a story which again illustrated this particular species of *hillul Hashem*. I find it difficult to speak about the subject because it always pains me to criticize other Jews in public, certainly Orthodox Jews, and most certainly my colleagues in the Orthodox rabbinate. Nonetheless, my conscience impels me to do so, because where the divine Name is desecrated, one must not keep silent even if it entails speaking out against one's teachers or colleagues.

According to the news report, a coalition of Orthodox rabbinic groups came out publicly against the proposed constitutional amendment granting equal rights to women. The coalition, which asserted it represented more than one half of the 2,500 Orthodox rabbis in the United States, explained that the amendment threatens Orthodox synagogues which separate men and women at services with a *meḥitza*; that it would jeopardize our "parochial schools" which keep separate programs for boys and girls; and that equal rights for women, as spelled out in the amendment, endanger morality in the whole of the United States.

Not being conversant with the science of statistics, I cannot state the exact degree of invalidity of the claim that this group represents more than half of the 2,500 Orthodox rabbis in the country. I was unaware that there are so many Orthodox rabbis in the United States, unless that number includes rabbis serving in every form of trade, profession, and business. Certainly, I would deny that the majority of pulpit rabbis, who feel a personal and professional responsibility for the destiny of Torah in this country, subscribe to their views. And, lest silence be interpreted as consent, let me make it clear to this congregation that this "coalition" does not represent me and the great majority of my colleagues and teachers in the rabbinate.

This group feels that the proposed amendment threatens Orthodox practice. I personally do not believe that it does or will, simply because religion and church are essentially separated in this country. Nevertheless, to the degree that this apprehension is valid, there is legitimate ground for preparing our defense in the courts. But to oppose the amendment on the grounds that equal rights will increase immorality is to jeopardize the cause of morality! It is primarily geared to the economics of this country. The sponsors of the amendment demand that women of equal competence with men should be compensated equally with men. It has nothing to do with morality; and if it does, it is morality that would demand that this right be granted and the source of economic discrimination be removed. It will simply not do to say, as one of the spokesmen of this coalition did in the news report, that those women who maintain that they do not have equal rights are arrogant, and women should be feminine and not arrogant. Is arrogance really less offensive when it is a man who practices it than when it is a woman?

I am troubled too by the reference to "parochial schools." The same rabbinic spokesman asserted that in our "parochial schools" (i.e., yeshivot or day schools), boys receive "deeper academic study, while the girls focus on steno, typing, and dietary observance in the home."

This does not speak for the majority of the day schools in this country. Where Orthodox parents prefer that their girls not pursue academic careers, that is their privilege. It should be pointed out that they do not permit their boys as well to go on to advanced secular education.

But our interpretation of Orthodox Judaism is not necessarily the same as that of these parents. I am personally opposed to co-education beyond the lower grades, but more on psychological and educational than religious grounds – certainly not because of some purported intellectual deficiency on the part of the female of the species. If I approve of a difference in curriculum, it is only because of the relevance to their later interests and concerns. But our girls get a Jewish education through high school, through college (where Stern College for Women was especially built for this purpose), and through the post-graduate levels up to the doctorate in Yeshiva University and other schools. I have personally encouraged as many bright young women to go on to higher Jewish studies and their PhDs as I have discouraged young men from doing so because they would be going beyond their depth. It simply makes no sense to speak of girls being inadequate to intellectually demanding tasks in an age when girls are learning nuclear physics, engaging in medical research, becoming knowledgeable in the mysteries of economics, and where two of the most embattled nations in the world, including Israel, are headed by women, whose popularity seems to be far greater than that of the president of the greatest country in the world.

Typing and steno are honorable professions. Anyone who runs an office can appreciate their importance and the need for talented and responsible personnel in these fields. But it is ludicrous to make of secretarialism a new dogma of a Jewish sectarianism.

At the same time I would like clearly to affirm our Orthodox position on separate seating and *meḥitza* in the synagogue, and especially as opposed to the extravagant reaction of the Reform rabbi in the article of *The New York Times* the day following.

Torah regards men and women as being of equal metaphysical value – for the value of human beings in the first place derives from their creation in the "image of God," and both men and women were created in this divine image. However, equality of value does not imply identity of function. Men and women have different functions in life, and that is the way it ought to be. This difference in function is reflected in the differing conception of their roles by the *Halakha*. There are those who maintain that "separate but equal" has been ruled as inherently unequal by the Supreme Court. That may be so, but the Supreme Court is not the supreme arbiter of Jewish philosophy and *Halakha*. Furthermore, while this may be true with regard to the races, for there is no reason why they should function differently, it certainly is not valid with regard to the sexes, where differences in function are perfectly understandable and right. It is true that the current movement for the reassessment of male and female roles may be quite correct in showing us that we may have erred in the functions we previously assigned as rigidly belonging to either males or females. But unquestionably, despite the extravagant and often ludicrous claims of Women's Lib, there are and should be and always will be different functions, for in a world of "unisex" both men and women will ultimately suffer.

The principle of separate seating in the synagogue must not be thought of as representing any claim of inequality or inferiority. Its purpose is to remove the distraction that may come because of erotic stimulation. If the purpose of coming to a synagogue is for American Jews to indulge in a kind of social ritual of self-identification as Jews, then there certainly is no reason for men and women to sit separately. But that is not our conception of prayer. For us, *tefilla* is the presentation of oneself before God, the focusing and concentration of all our thoughts on the One before whom we stand, and hence any distraction must be banished. The ideal for prayer, so conceived, is holiness; and the bane of holiness is eroticism.

I will make no attempt to quote, selectively, occasional passages from our long literature showing the superiority of women. There is no use in citing stray *ma'amrei Ḥazal,* for they can prove both the superior and the subordinate status of women. You can find almost any opinion of women in a literature which has lasted over 2,500 years and the quotations of perhaps a thousand different individuals. The point is that there is nothing within the *Halakha* on synagogue structure that has to do with difference in value, with inferiority or superiority.

Yet, if I am to be frank – and honesty permits me nothing less than that – I must state that we do have problems. We have not yet worked out sufficiently all the issues dealing with the role of women in Judaism. (The Jewish community and Jewish philanthropy have unfortunately not been sufficiently farsighted to organize the kind of think-tanks that will allow Jewish scholars, presently overburdened beyond their capacities, to devote themselves to this and other such problems with sufficient leisure and scholarship.) There are times when Jewish law does reveal what seems to be a discriminatory attitude against women. What we must do is research and find out to what extent such problems can be ameliorated. If we should find that the contemporary standards of fairness and equality are contravened by the basic halakhic view on the role of the sexes, then we shall have to take our stand with Torah, clearly and unambiguously, in the faith that the innate rightness of Torah and its moral justice will not only prevail, but will come to be appreciated and vindicated in the course of time. Torah was meant for the ages, while the criteria and tastes of each age rise only to fade away into obsolescence.

But I do not believe that enough has yet been done to elaborate a halakhic view that will consider all aspects of the problem, old and new, and that will take advantage of the full range of halakhic remedies available to us.

So we do have problems, and at such time it ill behooves us to attack others, and at the same time expose ourselves to even greater attacks by them.

As if things were not bad enough with the abominable public image of Orthodox Jewry in this country, there are the pickets of Hasidim against Golda Meir in this country and the proclamation by a *rosh yeshiva* discouraging or forbidding *aliya* because of Women's National Service in Israel – as if all of these things were not bad enough in the way they paint the picture of Orthodoxy, we now have this intemperate, injudicious, and extravagant statement, in the name of the majority of Orthodox rabbis in America!

These people have kicked the *Shekhina* up to the highest heaven. They have made Torah Judaism appear as exotic and alien, as remote and intolerant and benighted. What a *ḥillul Hashem*!

We have, as I have stated, a problem both in the application and in the interpretation of Torah to the present generation. There always were problems of this kind; there are, and there always will be, because that is the nature of Torah and its applicability. But if we do not have an adequate answer that will prove satisfactory, then let us be wise and keep silent. There was a great Talmudist, Rabbi Joseph Dov Soloveitchik of Brisk, who was known to have said: "Not everything that one thinks ought he to say, not everything that he says ought he to write down, and not everything that he writes ought he to print."

I therefore disagree with both extremes. One extreme feels that "relevance" is the only criterion of religion, and that therefore Torah must always be "with it," that every new fad must be accepted as the latest dictate of modernity, and that we must make efforts to show that Judaism not only now but always has anticipated this point of view. Such super-modernistic apologetics are not only unobjective and untrue, they are downright silly. The opposite extreme is equally dangerous. There seems to be a tendency on the part of some Orthodox rabbis, in reaction against the "relevance" kick, to show that Torah always opposes modern culture and tastes and sensitivities. In order to show this, they seem to feel that it is necessary to paint Torah in the most benighted colors, to make Judaism appear as impossible of achievement and to make certain that no one of culture or learning will want to have anything to do with it. I never understand why some of our brethren seem to be beset by suicidal drives, by a kind of collective spiritual masochism.

This unfortunate publicity has not served us well. It will accomplish nothing for the legal defense of our status, but will give the impression that we are far away and far out, as if the *Shekhina* is in the seventh heaven, and Orthodox Jews out of this world, and the *Halakha* inaccessible and unattractive.

This is not the way of Torah, about which it is written (Proverbs 3:17), "Its ways are the ways of pleasantness and all its paths peace." This is not our *derekh* or the *derekh haYahadut*. Our "way" is to make God rejoice "as on the day that heaven and earth were created"; to bring Him down to earth, into close rapport with mankind; to make Torah appear in its most attractive form. It is our task to speak out courageously and bravely when Torah offers a judgmental criticism of our contemporary standards and deeds, but, at the same time, to show how it can be fulfilling and enlightening to men and women in all ages.

When one acts so that Torah appears primitive and unjust and infinitely removed, he is irresponsible and is in violation of the great transgression of the desecration of God's Name.

Our task is to invoke God, to appeal to Him to come down to us. "The Lord is close to all those who call upon Him" (Psalms 145:18). He will certainly respond – but under one condition: only to those who call upon Him *"be'emet,"* with truth and sincerity, with honesty and sensitivity.

Tazria-Metzora

Aspects of Creativity[1]

The most wondrous miracle in the course of life is the appearance of life itself – the birth of a child. If, therefore, when a child is born, he or she is greeted with *simḥa*, with happiness, this is as it should be – for a child is the very highest expression of joyous creativity. No wonder the Jewish tradition teaches us that the father and mother of a child are partners with God in His creation – for the act of childbirth is the most significant creative act in human life. According to some of our classical commentators, the meaning of the biblical verse that man was created in the image of God (Genesis 1:26) means that just as God is creative so does man have the capacity to build and create. The most God-like of all human activities is that of creativity.

It is interesting therefore, and somewhat perplexing, to note the somewhat remarkable law which comes at the beginning of the first of the two portions which we read this morning, namely, that a woman is considered in a state of ritual impurity, or *tuma*, for a specified period of time after childbirth. If, indeed, the creative act is an imitation of God,

---

1. April 27, 1963.

65

why should the act of childbirth, the most creative natural act of which a human being is capable, bring with it, as a side-effect, a state of *tuma*?

What the Torah wanted to teach us, thereby, is that every creative human act, no matter how noble, inevitably brings with it certain negative features. Destructivity is one of the aspects of creativity, for creativity is a reorientation of the *koḥot hanefesh*; it disturbs the equilibrium of the inner workings of the soul, for what is new can be produced only by upsetting the status quo (this idea has been elaborated psychoanalytically by Freud in *Civilization and its Discontents*), and from the same reorganization which produces creative results there also emerge destructive consequences. You cannot have *yetzira* (creativity) without *tuma*. The creative act involves an area of shade, something negative, an element of pain and agony and frustration. The seed must rot for the plant to grow. When you carve wood, you must expect splinters. The sculptor must chip away part of the block and discard it in order to have the figure, which his imagination has conceived, emerge.

In the very creation of the world, according to the Kabbala, the same principle held true; the Creation was accompanied by what the Kabbala called the "*shevirat hakeilim*," the breaking or bursting of vessels – meaning that just as God gave life and vitality to all the world in His holiness, so did some of this life-giving holiness become entrapped and ensconced in evil. God gave rise to the world, and, as a side-effect, there arose evil as well. *Tuma*, uncleanliness, accompanied the cosmic act of *yetzira*.

The establishment of great nations, great ideas, and great institutions likewise follows this pattern. American democracy came into being at the expense of bloodshed and revolution. French democracy, a most creative element in world history, carried with it the *tuma* of Robespierre and the symbol of the guillotine. The people of Israel were created in the house of slavery of Egypt. And when we left, there came along with us the *eirev rav*, the riffraff, those who did not deserve integration into our people. It is they who, according to the Jewish tradition, were responsible for the making of the golden calf and all the other sordid features that characterized the history of our people in those early days. No creation is possible without an element of impurity.

That is why the Torah gives us, in this week's *sidra*, the laws of impurity as they relate to the *yoledet*, the mother who has just given birth to a child. The Torah wishes to inform us, by observing the most creative of all acts, childbirth, that every element of *yetzira* has the adhesions of impurity, teaching us thereby to expect them and thus avoid their negative consequences.

Parenthood itself contains risks of impurity. Some parents imagine that their children belong to them, and fail, even in later years, to allow a child to develop as an independent personality – even as some parents fail in the opposite direction, by abandoning responsibility for guiding and directing a child through being overly permissive. How many parents really feel they have completely succeeded in raising their children without making any mistakes? In order to prepare young parents to expect mistakes, and to try to avoid them, the Torah stresses *tuma* right after childbirth.

Thus too it reminds the person building a business that if he does not take care, he is liable to build the business at the cost of his ethical integrity, or at the expense of psychological tranquility. That person may become so totally involved in his work that other aspects of his personality wither away. It warns the person in public life that he may create a great deal of good for the community, but if he is not aware of the principle of *tuma* that adheres to creativity, he may neglect his family while paying exclusive attention to the larger human or national community. It warns the writer or the novelist that in the throes of creation and in the intense dedication necessary to produce something of enduring value, he is liable to disturb the inner recesses of the soul and to allow repressed demons to emerge; he may thus end up ignoring moral responsibilities as an artistic creator. All too often modern writers, sometimes Jews more than others, allow their literary creations to wallow in all kinds of obscenity, all sorts of verbal *tuma*.

Perhaps this too is the explanation of the remarkable law in this week's *sidra*, that the mother's period of impurity is twice as long upon the birth of a baby girl as upon the birth of a baby boy. The question of this difference in time span intrigued our Rabbis of old. When the question was asked in the Talmud (*Nidda* 31b), the answer given was, enigmatically, that when a boy is born everyone rejoices, and therefore seven days of impurity is sufficient. But when a girl is born, there is an element of sadness, and therefore the impurity lasts twice as long.

But what does this mean? Surely not every parent always wants a boy and not a girl – ordinary experience proves that. Even in the antiquity, it was recognized that the human race could not survive without the female portion of its population.

The Maharsha, the famed commentator on the Talmud, explains this as follows: When a girl is born, the mother in her own pain and agony of childbirth realizes that this young infant will someday have to undergo the same excruciating experience, and therefore, despite all her happiness at the gift God has given her, she is already saddened because her daughter will have to repeat the same experience.

I would prefer to interpret that just a bit differently. Because creativity implies impurity, therefore the greater the creation, the longer and more intense the period of impurity; the greater the light, the more marked is the shadow. When it comes to this most significant of all examples of natural creativity, it is the female of the species who is more creative; it is she who gives birth, not the male. Therefore, when a daughter is born, the creative act is at its greatest and most intense, for a woman has given birth to a child who herself possesses the capacity for human creativity – in other words, the ability to give birth to yet another generation in its own time. Because the birth of a daughter is so much more a creative act than the birth of a son, the period of impurity is twice as great for the mother. Hence, the additional length of the period of *tuma* is not an indication of the relative value of a son or a daughter as such, but, quite to the contrary, a commentary on the greater creativity-value the Torah ascribes to womanhood.

It is with these thoughts in mind that our hearts turn in gratitude to the Almighty for having given us, fifteen years ago, the gift of the State of Israel at such a crucial point in the history of our people.

The State of Israel was the most creative achievement of our people, in a national sense, in the last two thousand years. Not only is the State itself the creation of the people of Israel, but this creation itself possesses the potential of further creativity in generations to come. It is truly *bat Tzion* – the "daughter of Zion." And the idea we have been expressing, that creativity inevitably has a proportionate aspect of impurity, should be for us both a source of solace and a warning.

All of us who love the State of Israel and admire it and are thankful to Heaven for it, accept it as an immensely creative contribution to the life of our people. And yet anyone who refuses to surrender his critical faculties will be able to find negative features in the life of the State. Certainly it is by no means the messianic goal and the fulfillment of the thousands of years of striving, dreaming, hoping, and prophesying of our people. The religious complexion of the State is by no means stable, and not yet that which we have prayed and hoped for. The creation of the State resulted in a sudden lessening of the idealistic fervor which brought it into being. There are other areas of shade that one can find.

What our *sidra* of today tells us is that this is to be expected, and that it would be completely unnatural were such a historically creative act not to have a concomitant of "impurity" – and that if we are aware of this, we can look for these elements of *tuma* and rid ourselves of them.

How can we dispose of this spiritual impurity, this residue of *galut* that has come along into the free State of Israel from the many lands of our dispersion?

The answer is by following the same pattern that the Torah described for the purification of the *yoledet*, she who gave birth.

One element is time: The Torah specifies a number of days, no more, no less. You can't hurry up the process. You simply have to wait. Anyone who expects or expected that the State of Israel would suddenly come into being as a full-fledged messianic state was simply daydreaming and completely out of touch with reality. It will take time until impurities that have attached themselves to us during the last 100 years that Jewish souls have wandered off into the labyrinthine channels of strange ideals and systems are gone, and the *tuma* is spent, and the population of the State of Israel is ready for a great period of reawakening and *teshuva*. Nothing can hurry that natural process of maturation and purification.

The second element is *tevila*, immersion, purposeful purification of ourselves. It means that we must consciously seek to wash away from ourselves all the accretions of alien ideologies that have disrupted the normal development of our spiritual life in the State of Israel and in the Diaspora as well. *"Ein Mayim ela Torah,"* "Water refers to Torah" (*Bava Kama* 17a). The waters of immersion, which the Torah prescribes for the mother who gave birth, symbolize the purification through Torah of the Jewish people throughout the world, they who are the mother of the State of Israel. All Jews can rid themselves of the spiritual impurity of our times not only by waiting for the natural process to take place, but also by dipping our souls into the waters of Torah and the "Sea of Talmud." We must return to our primordial spiritual origin and there cleanse our souls and our spirit and be prepared for the great purification of the people of Israel in the great and glorious future ahead of us.

The beloved President of Israel, Yitzhak Ben Zvi, who passed away this week, represented both these elements. He was, first, a leader of infinite patience, a forbearing father of his people in whose presence all tempers were stilled and troubled spirits calmed. And, second, he had a love for Torah and a deep reverence for its scholars. He was a synagogue-Jew, a student of Talmud, and an *oheiv Yisrael*, a lover of Israel. He represented an element of *tahara* – of purity and purification in the life of the fledgling state. May his blessed soul return pure to its Creator.

And so our hearts turn to the Almighty in prayer that He guide the State of Israel and her leaders in the right path; that He send consolation to her grieving citizens; that He protect her from her many enemies so ominously surrounding her from all sides; that He purify her spiritual life with the pure waters of Torah, and allow all of us to "draw the waters joyously from the wells of salvation" (Isaiah 12:3).

God, Man, and State[1]

The conjunction of the two *sidrot* we read today, *Tazria* and *Metzora*, is remarkable. The first speaks of birth, the second of a kind of death (a leper is considered partially dead; see *Nedarim* 64b). *Tazria* describes the joyous acceptance into the fold of a new Jew by means of *brit mila*, circumcision, while *Metzora* tells of the expulsion of the leper from the community.

Yet, these two portions are read on the same Shabbat with no interruption between them. The tension between these two opposites, this dialectic between birth and death, between pleasure and plague, between rejoicing and rejecting, speaks to us about the human condition as such and the existence of the Jew specifically. Even more, this tension contains fundamental teachings of Judaism that are relevant to the problems of the State of Israel whose eighteenth birthday we shall be celebrating this Monday.

After delineating the laws of childbirth, the Torah in the first *sidra* gives us the laws of circumcision. The *Midrash Tanḥuma* (*Tazria* 7)

---

1. April 23, 1966.

71

relates a fascinating conversation concerning this Jewish law. We are told that Turnus Rufus, a particularly vicious Roman commander during the Hadrianic persecutions in Palestine, spoke to Rabbi Akiva, the revered leader of our people. He asked Rabbi Akiva: "Which is more beautiful: the work of God or the work of man?" Rabbi Akiva answered: "The work of man." Turnus Rufus was visibly disturbed by the answer. He continued: "Why do you circumcise your children?" Rabbi Akiva said: "My first reply serves as an answer to this question as well." Whereupon Rabbi Akiva brought before the Roman commander stalks of wheat and loaves of good white bread. He said to the Roman: "Behold, these are the works of God, and these are the works of man. Are not the works of man more beautiful and useful?" Said the Roman to Rabbi Akiva: "But if God wants people to be circumcised why are they not born circumcised?" Rabbi Akiva replied: "God gave the *mitzvot* to Israel *letzaref bahen*, to temper or purify His people thereby."

Here is the triumphant Roman commander, activist, arrogant, proud, and power-drunk. In an attitude of contempt, he faces the aged Jewish leader of this conquered people, a man who proclaims that the greatest principle of life is the study of Torah. What can these otherworldly mystics know about the world, about reality, about life? So he taunts the old rabbi: How come you circumcise your children? Do you not believe that man, as God's creation, is already born perfect?

But the Roman pagan is amazed by the response: No! All of Judaism – its philosophy, its Torah, its *mitzvot* – is based upon the premise that God withheld perfection from His creation, that He only began the task and left it to man, His *tzellem*, His image, to complete. In Genesis 2:3, we are taught that God rested from creating the world "which God created to do" – and Rabbi Samson Raphael Hirsch interpreted that to mean that God created the world for man "to do." Therefore, Rabbi Akiva shows Turnus Rufus the wheat stalks and the white breads to teach him that God has created wheat because He wants man to do something with it. It is God's will that human beings make the created world more beautiful and more perfect. No wonder that in the Jewish view science and technology play such a positive role. No wonder that religious Jewry has contributed so mightily, throughout the ages and today as well, to the advancement of science and the control of nature.

Therefore, too, the *mitzvot,* and especially circumcision, were revealed to Israel to teach that people must act in order to perfect themselves and the world, and in the process, *letzaref bahen,* to purify themselves and fulfill all their sublime potentialities.

Indeed, Rabbi Akiva himself exemplified this great principle. He was, on the one hand, one of the saintliest spirits in all our history. The Talmud, in imaginative grasp of the truth, tells us that when Moses ascended Mount Sinai to receive the Torah and he saw the sacred soul of Rabbi Akiva, he protested to God that Akiva was more worthy to be the bearer of Torah than he, Moses, was. And yet, on the other hand, it was the same Rabbi Akiva who did not isolate himself in the academy, but became the sponsor of Bar Kokhba, the great Jewish general who led the revolution against Rome.

This, then, is what *mila* teaches us: "The work of flesh and blood is beautiful indeed." The world is an uncompleted creation; man's fate is to finish it. This is the principle of activism. The State of Israel was built by people who perceived this Jewish principle. They were the ones who refused to stand aside, outside of the stream of history, but who actively took upon themselves to rebuild Jewish statehood. Their activity was in full keeping with the Jewish tradition as taught by the law of *mila.* More than enough Jewish blood was spilled in the effort, and the sweat and tears invested shall never be forgotten.

Yet, this is only half the story. There is an opposite danger. If man is indeed a creator, then there is the peril that he will become intoxicated with power and self-delusions, that he will begin boasting and bragging and proclaiming bombastically, "My own power and my own strength have performed all this" (Deuteronomy 8:17). When he circumcises his child, he tends to forget that a healthy child is the gift of God. When he bakes his bread, he does not always realize that the wheat came from God's earth. When he builds his state, he ignores the fact that without the divine promise to Abraham and divine guidance throughout the ages there would be no Jews to build the Jewish state. When he is self-completing, he tends to become, in his imagination, self-creating. He is self-finishing and thinks that he is therefore self-made; and God spare us from self-made men!

To help us avoid this dangerous delusion, we have the teachings of *Metzora.* Just as *Tazria* and *mila* warn us to avoid the passivism that issues from a misunderstanding of faith, so *Metzora* and the law of the banishing of the leper outside the camp teach us to avoid the fatal illusion that issues from faithlessness. Just as one *sidra* tells us to circumcise the flesh and assert our manhood, so the second tells us to circumcise the heart and serve our God.

The great medieval scholar Rabbi Elazar of Worms explains the law of *Metzora* and this banishment outside the camp by means of a comment on a famous verse in the Psalms (49:13), "Man abideth not in honor; he is like the beasts that perish." Man, says Rabbi Elazar, is born naked and ignorant, without understanding and intelligence. But God puts him on his feet, grants him wisdom and insight, feeds him and clothes him and makes him great. But then man forgets and does not understand that all this glory came to him from his God. Therefore, he becomes like a *beheima*, a mere animal. An animal is not kept at home, but sent out to pasture; he is unfit to live in a truly human community. So a person who forgets God is a *metzora*, is morally sick, and must be sent outside the camp of his or her peers. The leper symbolizes the individual who acquired self-confidence at the cost of fidelity to God and therefore is reduced to the role of a beast.

Mankind, then, must be co-creator with God. *Tazria* teaches that we must imitate our Maker; *Metzora* reminds us not to impersonate our God, not to be imposters. One *sidra* stresses the virtue of human commission, the other – the virtue of human submission to God.

Indeed, in an insight brimming with tremendous significance, the eminent Italian-Jewish thinker Rabbi Moshe of Trani finds this second principle in the commandment of *mila* itself. Just as circumcision teaches that man must act, so its particular designation for the eighth day teaches that his actions must not lead to the mere amassing of power and self-importance. Rather, man must acknowledge and reach out to the Creator of all the world. The number seven, Rabbi Moshe teaches, is the symbol of nature. Seven is the number of days in the week, the unit of time which establishes the rhythm of our lives. The earth, itself agricultural, follows a seven year cycle in Judaism – that of the *shemita*. The number seven, therefore, stands for this world in its fullness. The number eight, however, is beyond seven – it teaches that you must transcend what seven symbolizes, you must go beyond nature and reach out for the supernatural, for God, He who creates nature. Were *mila* on the seventh day, then the duty of man would be to correct the imperfections of Nature, but forever to stay within it as nothing more than a clever animal. But *mila* was commanded for the eighth day, to teach that the purpose of all man's activity, the purpose of his work on Nature, is to elevate himself beyond the perfection of body and mind, beyond the conquest of the world, beyond technology. When man controls his environment, he fulfills the number seven; when he controls his instincts, he reaches the number eight. His technology is symbolized by the number seven; his theology by eight. *Mila* on the eighth day teaches that man must not only complete himself but must grow beyond himself; he must yearn and aspire to something higher. It signifies not only *mila* but *brit*; not only a surgical cut, but the sign of the covenant, a contract with God sealed in blood. It means that if a human being will not strive to be more than human, he must become less than human, an animal: "He is like the beasts that perish" (Psalms 49:13). Then, man becomes a *metzora*, and like an animal, must be sent out "*ḥutz lamaḥaneh*," outside the camp of human beings.

Indeed, this is the crucial problem concerning the character of the State of Israel: Is it to be the symbol of seven, or the symbol of eight? Will it be just a natural state, or something higher, something nobler? If Israel will be only natural, a state like all others, a small sliver of real estate on the shores of the Mediterranean, considered nothing more than the creation of the Hagana and Sabra ingenuity, then it has no special claim on Jewish communities throughout the world – no more than its population warrants. It has no right to messianic pretenses. Such a conception places it *ḥutz lamaḥaneh*, outside the purview of authentic Jewish history, an aberration. It is then in defiance of the covenant; it is the way of *tuma*, impurity. Only by fulfilling the symbol of eight, of loyalty to the covenant of God, of Torah, does it go the way of *tahara*, of purity and rebirth, of joyous fulfillment of the historic dreams and prayers and prophecies of our history.

This, then, is the real problem on this eve of the eighteenth birthday of the State of Israel: Will it be *mila* or *brit*? Surgery or covenant? *Tazria* or *Metzora*? *Tahara* or *tuma*? Striving to be more than a natural human political entity, or falling to a mere natural group which, under the impress of secular nationalism, often becomes beastly ("he is like the beasts that perish")?

Such decisions are never made all at once. They involve long processes measured in historic time, certainly more than eighteen years. Many facts will determine the answer, and not the least of them will be the spiritual leadership in the state under the resolute stewardship of our distinguished and revered guest, His Eminence, Chief Rabbi Unterman,[2] may he live and be well. Their enormously difficult task is to be both responsive to their fellow Israelis and responsible to our Heavenly Father. Like the *kohanim* in our *sidra*, they must confront all Jews, the perfectly pure and perilously impure. Sometimes it is their unhappy and tragic task to say to a man: "*tamei*," "You are impure – you must go out!" Yet their greater and nobler task is to teach this same *tamei* to return, to bring Jews back into the historic community of Israel, to train all Jews in the way of the Torah's *tahara*. It is by no means a simple duty; it is, in fact, unenviably difficult. Our hopes and good wishes and our prayers for divine guidance and blessings go to Chief Rabbi Unterman and his distinguished colleagues in this historic mission.

We have spoken of *brit mila* in relation to the State of Israel. The eighteenth birthday also has another significance – "*shemone esrei lehuppa*" (*Avot* 5:22), the eighteenth year is traditionally the year of marriage. Let us conclude then by extending our wishes to Israel in a manner appropriate to both events. Let us all wish the State of Israel divine blessings – *leTorah lehuppa ulema'asim tovim*. May it be a future of Torah in which Israel will accept the divine word and turn to its Father in Heaven. May it be the time of *huppa*, the marriage of hearts between Israel and Jews throughout the world. And then, having returned to God and to Jews throughout the world, may Israel become the shining beacon of *ma'asim tovim*, of good deeds and noble living, throughout the world and for all mankind – *leTorah lehuppa ulema'asim tovim, amen.*

---

2. Rabbi Isser Yehuda Unterman was the Ashkenazi Chief Rabbi of Israel from 1964 to 1972.

The Varieties of Vulgarity[1]

According to tradition (*Arakhin* 16a), the terrible plague (*nega*) of *tzara'at* (usually mistranslated as "leprosy") is occasioned by one of three sins. Amongst them is that of *gassut*, to which we shall devote this morning's talk.

Gassut means thickness, heaviness, and therefore crudity or rudeness or obtuseness. In a word, *gassut* is vulgarity.

It does not require unusual wisdom or perceptiveness to observe that our society suffers from an over-abundance of vulgarity. We need but look about ourselves to notice the obvious lack of refinement and delicacy and sensitivity. Indeed, not only does *gassut* lead to *nega'im*, but today vulgarity itself is a veritable plague.

Modern life, for all its sophistication, tends towards vulgarity. Possibly it is a result of our liberal, democratic tradition. Any democratizing movement tends on the one hand to bring culture and the "finer things of life" to the masses of the people, but on the other hand also lower standards and debases the coin of culture. This is true of

---

1. May 4, 1968.

language which becomes vulgarized and of music and art which tend to deteriorate with the increase in mass education. Perhaps the preponderance of vulgarity is the result of instantaneous electronic communication, so that an eruption of vulgarity in any one part of the world, especially America, is immediately broadcast by satellite to all parts of the world which regard such conduct as the norm of behavior.

But certainly, vulgarity, as the very word indicates, tends towards commonness; it spreads like the plague. *Gassut* is itself a species of *nega'im*. It is not because a thing is common or popular that, by itself, makes it vulgar. We are not and should not be snobbish. But vulgarity, as an inadequate conception of the art of living, simply happens to characterize most people; for the art of living is one that is not easy to master.

Let us be more analytic. We can, I believe, discern three varieties of *gassut*, of vulgarity.

Lexicographers tell us that the word *gass* usually appears in conjunction with one of three words: *leiv, ruaḥ,* and *da'at,* that is, heart, spirit, and knowledge or mind.

Gassut haleiv is emotional impudence and grossness, or arrogance.

Gassut haruaḥ is the crudity of the spirit, or spiritual insensitivity.

Gassut hada'at is obtuseness of the mind, or the failure of intellectual discrimination.

The first of these is arrogance, *gassut haleiv,* or emotional vulgarity. This species of vulgarity dulls a person's sense of humor and makes him lose all perspective about his place in the world. Such a person cannot distinguish between self-worth and inflated bombast, whereby only he is important and no one else is. The person of *gassut haleiv,* vulgarity, is so confident of his own superiority that he considers himself part of the "in crowd" and will be seen with no one else; therefore God brings upon such a person the plague of *tzara'at* which requires that that individual be banished "*ḥutz lamaḥaneh,*" outside the camp. The person who wanted to be only "in" is now "out," literally an outcast. Indeed, God refuses to abide such an individual in His own *maḥaneh,* His very world, for the Lord says concerning such a person: "The world is too small for the both of us" (*Sota* 5a); that individual and I cannot co-exist in one world. This makes sense. The arrogant person, the person of emotional vulgarity, suffers from a swollen ego, one which displaces not only fellow men from the scene of his existence, but which tends to push God Himself out of the world. That person's punishment therefore is a just retaliation – God pushes such an individual out of His world.

But the bluster of such vulgarity of heart, as we know today, usually is a cover for an inner void, an inner emptiness. One who suffers from what appears to be an excess of superiority usually is painfully aware of his inferiority, for which he is actually quite ashamed.

This, I believe, is at the bottom of the insight of the Talmud which tells us that a man of *gassut halev*, or arrogance, is considered by the Holy One as if he had worshiped an idol (*Sota* 4b). This is the accepted reading in our text of the Talmud. But a variant, recorded by the disciple of Maimonides, Rabbi Joseph ben Judah Ibn Aknin, in his *Sefer HaMussar*, says that such a person is considered by the Holy One as if he himself were a veritable idol! An idol has all the appearance of life but is really dead. The man of arrogance and bombast and vanity tries to impress you with his superiority, but such superiority is indeed non-existent. We recall what King David said about the idols: "Eyes they have, but they see not; they have ears but they hear not" (Psalms 135:16-17). The one who suffers from the vulgarity of vanity has all the apparent appurtenances of personality, but none of the underlying reality. This kind of vulgarian appears sociable, when that person is really gathering gossip with which he will be able to derogate others and thereby enhance his own ego. Such a person appears to be engaged in friendly conversation, but is really prattling in a monologue, concerned only with that which aggrandizes his own self. Such a person appears to look at you and listen to you, but "eyes they have, but they see not; they have ears but they hear not" – his ego blinds him to anything save that which concerns his own welfare. Such a person appears to be polite but his "please" is nothing more than servile begging and his "thank you" is an insincere down payment on favors he has yet to request. The vain individual is indeed vulgar!

The second variety of vulgarity is *gassut haruah*, spiritual obtuseness or insensitivity. In a word, it is the failure to appreciate the relations of values, to understand that all values are limited in time and place, that at the right occasion they are completely qualified and proper, but that at the wrong time and place they are grotesque and absurd. Therefore, the person of spiritual vulgarity suffers from distortion of values.

Indeed, what inspired the theme of this sermon is a particular species of spiritual vulgarity which reappears annually and never fails to irritate me with a special form of abhorrence. I refer to the advertisements which regularly appear in our press every year before Passover advising us to hurry and make our reservations in the various resort hotels where, we are told, a Passover vacation can be combined with a marvelous night club, where a famous cantor will entertain us at the same time that great bands will give us fun, where double choirs and heated indoor swimming pools all go together. Often I pray that these tasteless and insipid advertisements would remove one line from their text – "Dietary laws observed."

I admit that because of them I am embarrassed before gentiles, I am embarrassed before the Almighty, I am embarrassed before my very self.

A higher form of spiritual vulgarity afflicts American Jews, especially Orthodox ones, who misconstrue the very nature of the synagogue, who believe that it is a mark of honor and distinction to act in the synagogue as one acts in his very home, for it indicates that we are "at home" in the precincts of the House of God. Thus, we violate every norm of conduct that the *Halakha* demands of us in the synagogue, the standards of reverence for a holy place, and we excuse our irreverence by "*heimishkeit*" – a fabrication and a distortion of the *Halakha* and of all Judaism. It is a species of spiritual vulgarity to subvert the nature of the synagogue by being long on conversation and short on dress in it. Such empty prattle and constant chatter is a vulgarization of the spirit of holiness of a synagogue; and revealing too much of one's self because of fashion reveals as well a short-sightedness and a lack of spiritual and intellectual integrity which should impel us to leave such fashions outside the synagogue.

A still more subtle form of *gassut haruah* is the whole American Jewish attitude to the synagogue. American Jews often consider the "Temple" the center of all of Judaism. Now, a synagogue certainly is important. But it is never by any means more important than Shabbat or *kashrut* or family purity or ethical relations, and especially not more than the study of Torah. In Jewish law the academy of study is of greater sanctity than the house of prayer. I have always maintained that religious Jews in Israel have much to learn from American Orthodoxy, for we have undergone certain kinds of experiences of modernity, and Israelis can very well benefit by the lessons we have derived from these experiences. But in one sense we have much to learn from Israeli Jews. For in Israel, once a man is a truly committed religious Jew, he understands much better the value of the study of Torah than we do. In Israeli synagogues, for all their faults, you will find people attending lectures in Talmud and Torah with much greater regularity and greater numbers than you will in America.

Another subtle form of spiritual vulgarity, of *gassut haruah*, deserves our attention. This too deals with the exaggeration of values when they are out of place. There is a remarkable statement in the Talmud: *"Siman legassut haru'ah aniyut"* (*Shabbat* 33a) – poverty is a symptom of spiritual vulgarity. Did the Rabbis really mean to be so harsh on poor people? What they intended, I submit, is that the poor person is afflicted not only by being economically deprived and financially disadvantaged. An even greater tragedy derives from the psychological fact that inwardly such an individual begins to attribute extravagant powers to money. If only I had money, he begins to believe, all my problems would be solved. Money becomes to that person not something to attain in order to relieve certain difficulties, but it grows in his imagination into a veritable savior. This distortion of the value of money is a symptom of the disease of poverty, and it reveals itself in this spiritual vulgarity. The same is true not only for money but for social status or any other value.

The third variety of vulgarity is the intellectual form, *gassut hada'at* – the failure to discriminate between ideas, things, and people; the inability to comprehend conceptual subtleties.

As you know, on Saturday nights and on holiday nights, we add a paragraph in our *amida* prayer in which we speak of the separation, the *havdala*, between the sacred and the profane, between weekday and Sabbath or holiday. This particular passage is included in the fourth blessing, that in which we ask God for the gift of knowledge and intelligence. Why so? Because, the Talmud (*Yerushalmi Berakhot* 5:2) answers,

"Without knowledge, there can be no *havdala*," no discrimination, no differentiation. The major function of intelligence is analytic – to distinguish between various ideas. The failure to make such distinctions is, therefore, a form of *gassut hada'at*, a thickness of the mind, an obtuseness of intellect, or conceptual vulgarity.

The most distressing recent example of such *gassut hada'at* comes to us from the exalted chambers of the United Nations. I refer to the protest in the press in the UN against a recent parade by the State of Israel through old Jerusalem in celebration of Israel's twentieth anniversary as a state.

Now, one may legitimately question if this is the best way for Israel to celebrate its Independence Day. I confess that I have serious doubts as to whether it is in the spirit of Jewish history and Israeli tradition to celebrate such a great event exclusively by a military parade and showing off tanks and jet airplanes. I suspect that there is more that can be done which conforms better to the spirit of Israel and World Jewry.

Moreover, objective editorialists have a right to criticize Israel on the grounds that such a parade may have jeopardized the peace, although I totally disagree and feel that nothing of the sort is true.

However, has the UN the right to criticize Israel and "deplore" this parade? And has Mr. U Thant the moral right to be as active as he was in objecting to the parade?[2] Where was Mr. U Thant when Nasser massed his troops on the Sinai desert just about one year ago? Why did we hear no protest from the Secretary General of the UN when Nasser ordered UN troops to be pulled out of Sharm el Sheikh? Why was he silent when Jordanian artillery rained fire and death on Jerusalem? Why is he, and the entire UN, silent when the El Fatah terrorists infiltrate into Israel to kill men, women, and children? Can the UN not distinguish between terrorism and a peaceful parade, which will be held – indeed, was held – without the Damascus-type incendiary rhetoric and terrorism aimed at killing indiscriminately?

Clearly, this is a case of *gassut hada'at*, of vile intellectual vulgarity. And, of course, it is at its worst not a failure of intellect as much as

---

2. U Thant served as the Secretary-General of the United Nations from 1961 to 1971.

a willful intellectual obfuscation that issues from what at bottom is *gassut haru'ah*, spiritual vulgarity. For the UN has become a convention of people who speak in moral categories and intend only political issues. Perhaps it ought to be primarily a place of political confrontation – but it is vulgar to clothe political stratagems in moral terms.

Vulgarity – whether emotional, spiritual, or intellectual – is indeed a plague which infects young and old, in places high and low, in circles Jewish and non-Jewish. In this sense of its widespread character, *gassut* is really vulgar – it is common, it is ordinary.

No wonder every morning, almost immediately upon arising, we ask God, in our morning blessings, to let us be popular and respected and acclaimed by all those whom we meet: "Give us this day and every day the charm and grace and favor in Your eyes and in the eyes of all those who behold us." In a word – we want to be accepted by the masses.

But this involves a danger. If we are going to appeal to all those whom we meet, if we are going to pander to the taste and judgment of the lowest common – the most common – denominator, then we indeed may very well become the victims of vulgarity!

Therefore, we immediately continue our prayers: "May it be Your will, O Lord my God and God of my fathers, that You save this day and every day from impudent people and from impudence within ourselves...from any evil and disconcerting confrontation, whether with Jew or non-Jew." In short – spare us, O Lord, from the bitter encounter with vulgarity, in any form and manner, in any variety or of any people.

For the plague of vulgarity, in all its varieties, is the most pernicious of all.

And the only way of avoiding it is to remember that while there is nothing wrong in wanting to be popular and accepted and acclaimed by all the circles of our acquaintance, it is still more important to strive for favor in the eyes of God more than in the eyes of our fellow human beings.

Aḥarei Mot

The Normal Jew[1]

In this morning's *sidra* the Torah presents us with its code of sexual morality, a code that has been accepted as a cornerstone of our Western civilization.

However, despite the widespread acceptance in theory of the Torah's moral code, statistics in recent years indicate that it is honored more in the breach than in the observance. Moral laxity and marital infidelity have become part of a matter-of-fact way of life, not only amongst the idols of the amusement world, but for an ever larger number of people. The most corrosive aspect of this situation is what it has done to the morale of those who are truly moral. Since they are in the minority, or a gradually diminishing majority, they tend to think that perhaps they are wrong. Perhaps unchastity is normal, and those who abstain are not normal. Maybe, as some statisticians have suggested, our whole moral code needs revamping. Since much of what has been previously condemned as immoral and degenerate is now widely practiced, perhaps they should no longer be regarded as wrong and reprehensible.

---

1. April 28, 1962.

It is against this devious kind of reasoning that the Torah, centuries ago, proclaimed in clear words, in its introduction to its moral code, the doctrine, "Like the doings of the land of Egypt, wherein you dwelt, shall you not do; like the doings of the land of Canaan, whither I am bringing you, shall you not do; neither shall you walk in their statutes" (Leviticus 18:3). What the Torah is saying is what is being done – whether in Egypt or Canaan – is no guide for what should be done – whether in those places or anywhere else.

A distinguished man of letters, Joseph Wood Krutch, in his collected essays titled *Human Nature and the Human Condition*, has brilliantly analyzed the difference between two concepts which are most pertinent to our discussion. They are the concepts of "average" and "normal."

A new phenomenon in our modern age – with its democratization, its penchant for measuring and statistics, and its mass culture – is the tendency to identify the normal with the average, to believe that what most people do must be right. The sophisticated call this "relativism." The ordinary man knows it by experience as "being normal." To do as most people do – that is normal. To do otherwise – that is abnormal, or subnormal, as the case may be. When a young mother says, "I want my child to be normal," she usually – though not always – means that she does not want the child to stand out by being too bookish or too intellectual. She means "average," though she says "normal."

This is one of the most fundamental and disastrous errors that anyone can make. In order to remain civilized and prevent our whole society as well as our personal lives from deteriorating to the lowest common denominator, we must understand that there is a tremendous abyss that separates the average from the normal. The average is a description of what is; the normal is the ideal, the principle, what ought to be. It is only in a perfect world that the average is normal. In real life, the average is usually far below the normal. In fact, to be completely normal is very rare indeed.

From this it follows that it is the normal, not the average, which is desirable and for which we should strive. Otherwise, life becomes meaningless, even ludicrous. For instance, in the population at large there are some people who have only one leg, and some who have none. Thus the average man or woman has about 1.9 legs. Nevertheless, the normal person still has two legs. If we were to accept the popular error and say that what is average is normal, and that this is desirable, then anyone who has two legs ought to be required to cut off an inch of one of them! If the average is declared the normal, then all genius must be banished and the pursuit of excellence abandoned. All art must be reduced to cartooning, all music defined by the Hit Parade selections, and all literature confined to "Best Sellers."

This confusion of the two terms "average" and "normal" becomes most critical in the realm of morality. The statistics on the moral behavior of Americans, compiled and published in recent years, revealed a painful gap between the moral theories and immoral practices of great numbers of Americans. This in itself was simply a piece of astounding scientific information. The real problem arose when the report was interpreted – or misinterpreted, perhaps – to mean that these findings indicate a need for radically altering the moral code by which most Americans live. To conclude from these studies that our moral laws and standards should be modified in order to conform to our current practice – that is an assertion as immoral as anything described and tabulated in the reports themselves. To maintain that the normal must be made equal to the average is a most fundamental and unprincipled offense against decency. It implies that whatever one does is satisfactory, that he never need strive for any loftier goals, that mores may replace morals. Transpose this idea for immorality in America to murder in Germany and you have a perfect rationale for killing Jews under the Nazis – everyone is doing it, therefore it is proper or normal.

It is against this debased doctrine that the Torah, in introducing its moral legislation, warned us not to follow the practice of the Egyptians or the Canaanites, the "average" of the societies which we had left or to which we were coming, but the "normal" which, originating from Sinai, must continue unchanged and undiminished through the centuries.

It is interesting that Rashi (on Leviticus 18:3) maintains that the places in Egypt and Canaan where the Israelites dwelt and which the Torah condemns because of their immorality were the very worst, the most degenerate, of all the places in these two countries. The author of *Keli Yakar* takes exception to these comments by Rashi. Why, he asks, should Providence place the people of Israel, that nation which was to become the model of holiness and virtue before the world, specifically in those places least conducive to a moral life? On the contrary, he concludes, the areas inhabited by the Israelites were the least immoral of all.

The *Keli Yakar* has a good argument. And yet I believe that Rashi had greater insight. By placing the Jews in the most licentious of cities, Providence wanted to teach them, and civilized human beings of all generations, that reducing the normal to the average is not a harmless exercise. The average, that which is practiced by most people, is a fluctuating and uncertain standard. One who follows the morality of the average builds the foundation of his life on the quicksand of the spirit. The Torah says to our ancestors, and through them to us: If you want to see how low, how ugly, how degrading the average can become, look about you and observe how people lead their lives in a manner that can evoke nothing but disgust in any decent human being. If you are willing to enshrine the average as the normal, then you must be prepared to characterize as normal even degenerates if they happen to form the majority of any society. These most revolting of examples of the worst of the Egyptians and the Canaanites demonstrate the ultimate absurdity of taking refuge in the contemptible crowd.

What does it mean to be "normal?" The word derives from the Latin *norma* which in its anglicized form is "norm." This refers to a rule or authorized standard, a law. So that "normal" means "corresponding to a standard, conforming to law." The "average" is not law but statistics – it is the "doings" of the land of Egypt" and the "doings of the land of Canaan" – and concerning them we are commanded "*lo ta'asu*," do not follow or emulate this practice.

The Torah adds the words, "You shall not walk in their statutes." Why does the Torah first refer to "their doings," and then to "their statutes?" The famed Bible commentator Abraham Ibn Ezra remarks, "A man should not accustom himself to follow this way until it becomes for him a standard." In other words, Ibn Ezra tells us the Torah did not want us to sanction the average as the norm. The average must never be legitimatized as the standard conduct, the normal. For a Jew, the normal is not "the doings of the land of Egypt" or "the doings of the land of Canaan," but, as the Torah says in the very next verse, "And you shall observe My laws and My statutes." The law of God, that is our "norm." And the observance of that Torah – that is "normal," no matter how little the average individual may adhere to it.

Many of the modernist deviations from traditional Judaism also began with the principle that since the Law is largely violated, it loses its validity. This is arrant nonsense. If the average observance is low, it is the business of those who know and love the Torah to make the average rise until it becomes the normal, not the reverse. Torah is not an infinitely plastic substance that can constantly be changed so as to fit the shape of our taste and our conduct. It is we who must change and our circumstances that must be altered to fit the demands of Torah.

No wonder we read this portion, the *Parashat Arayot*, on Yom Kippur. On the very holiest day of the year we read the Torah's moral code, for on this day we pause and take stock and, doing that, we realize that we must apologize for being average – and promise to try to be normal.

What we have said is true not only about the Torah's moral legislation, but about all of life and all of the Torah. Thus, if you want to know who or what is a normal Jew, you cannot merely compile statistics and derive the answer. The sociologist can describe for you the average Jew. Only the student of Torah can tell you about the normal Jew. The average Jew today may not put on *tefillin*; the normal does. The average Jew may speak ill of another human being; the normal Jew – never. To be a normal Jew means to observe *kashrut*, the Sabbath, the laws of family purity – in short, all of Torah.

The average Jew today is subnormal, because he is far behind this kind of observance, this depth of commitment, this purity of mind and nobility of spirit. The normal Jewish child receives a full, maximal Jewish education, even if the average may achieve no more than a Sunday school scholarship. The State of Israel is a normal Jewish state when it is inspired and guided by the teachings of our Torah, the visions of our prophets, the doctrines of the Talmud. It is only another disappointingly average little country if it does not fulfill these requirements. When secular Zionism preached the establishment of a state *"kekhol hagoyim"*

(Deuteronomy 17:14), they called it a "normalization" of Jewish life. This was an historic error. Actually, it was a reduction to the average concept of most nations. It represents the "sub-normalization" of Jewish life.

This, then, is the duty of every individual, every society, every nation of the world itself – never to be smug and satisfied with the mere average, but to try to raise it to the levels of the objective norms which transcend the transient whims of men. For in this direction lies the enhancement and ennoblement of life itself. In the words of the Torah, immediately after urging us to abandon the practice of the averages of Egypt and Canaan and encouraging us to adopt the "normal" law of Torah, *"asher ya'aseh otam ha'adam vehai bahem"* (Leviticus 18:5) – for these are the statutes which a man shall do and live by them.

Something Different for a Change[1]

The problem of tradition versus innovation is an ancient, complex, and yet ever relevant one. The issue has never been fully resolved, and especially in Jewish life we must face it again in every generation.

When does conformity with accepted custom shade off from cautious conservatism to a rigid reactionary stand? And when does the willingness to experiment move one from the ranks of the liberals to those of the radicals who are contemptuous of the inherited values of the past? When is submission to tradition an act of moral cowardice and an evasion of responsibility, a cop-out on independent thinking? And when is the desire for change a thoughtless lust for cheap sensationalism and trivial thrill? These are questions of the greatest importance, and honorable men and women have and do differ about them.

It would be foolish to attempt an exhaustive analysis of the point of view of Judaism on this question, but is instructive to look for some insights from within the heritage of Judaism.

---

1. April 28, 1973.

A perusal of the first part of today's *sidra* impresses us with the Torah's powerful insistence upon observing every jot and title of the tradition. Thus, the Yom Kippur service of the High Priest in the Temple is set forth in the greatest detail, with constant and reiterated warnings that the slightest deviation from the prescribed ritual is a disaster, that any change is calamitous. Clearly, the Bible holds tradition and custom in the highest esteem.

And yet, here and there the Torah leaves us a hint which the Rabbis picked up and expanded, in order to complete the total picture by supplementing this valuation of tradition with another point of view. Thus, after describing the high point of Yom Kippur, when the High Priest has performed the service in the inner sanctum, we read, "And Aaron shall come to the Tent of Meeting and remove his linen garments which he wore when he came to the sanctuary, and he shall leave them there" (Leviticus 16:23). The Talmud (*Pesaḥim* 26a, and cited by Rashi) tells us that of the eight special garments that the High Priest wore for the Yom Kippur service, he was to remove four of them, those of white linen, and these required sequestering or burial. They could not be used again. He may not avail himself of these four garments on the following Yom Kippur.

Now, these priestly clothes were very costly linen garments. According to the *mishna* in *Yoma* (3:7), they were exceptionally expensive. Why, therefore, waste them? Why not put them aside for the following Yom Kippur? Why do not the Rabbis invoke the established halakhic principle (*Yoma* 39a) that, "The Torah is considerate of the material means of Israelites" and does not want to spend Jewish money unnecessarily?

An answer has been suggested by Rabbi Mordechai HaKohen. With all the concern of the Torah for the prescribed ritual and the unchanging tradition, the Torah very much wanted us to avoid the danger of routine. It considered boredom and rote as poison to the spirit and soul. Therefore, whereas we must follow every step of the ritual, the High Priest must have a change of garments every Yom Kippur, in the hope that the outward novelty will inspire and evoke from within the High Priest an inner freshness and enthusiasm, and that these four garments, which must always be different and always be new, will remain a symbol to all Israel that boredom is a slow death for the spirit, that only renewal can guarantee life. We need something different for a change!

What I think is the authentic Jewish view on our problem of tradition and change is this dual approach, insisting upon the unchanging framework of action, the fixed pattern of activity being transmitted from generation to generation without the slightest deviation, but demanding at the same time that inwardly we always bring a new spirit, a new insight, a new intuition into what we are doing. Objectively there is to be only tradition; subjectively there must always be something different, some change, something new. In outward practice custom prevails; in inner experience, only novelty and growth.

We find this emphasis on internal novelty in all the branches of the Jewish tradition. The *Halakha* itself, which is so insistent upon preserving outward form, cautions us against merely rote observance of *mitzvot* to which we habituate ourselves. It is very important for every man and woman to learn how to give religious expression to the various aspects of one's life, but never must this be done thoughtlessly and mindlessly merely because it has become second nature for us. Every year we perform the same *seder*, but our tradition challenges us to pour new meaning into the old form. Every Jewish wife and mother lights the candles on Friday afternoon in the same way every week of her life. It is her great opportunity to offer her own personal, even wordless, prayer to her Creator. But every week there should be some novelty, some additional requests, some new insights and concern – perhaps for someone else's family. When we offer the blessing on bread after a meal, we recite the same words, but perhaps sometimes we ought to vary the melody (if we do sing it) in order to challenge us to rethink our gratitude to the Almighty for being allowed to be included in that small percentage of humanity that suffers from overeating rather than under-eating. Every morning we recite the morning blessings. If we would really hear what we are saying, it is possible that our service would take three times as long! We bless God who is "*poke'aḥ ivrim*," who makes the blind see. Only a short while ago we were sleeping, completely sightless. Then we wake up and look at the world around us. We ought to marvel, we ought to be amazed and stunned, at the great miracle of being able to see!

Ask those who cannot, whose eyesight is impaired, or whose vision is threatened, and you will appreciate once again what it is to wake up every morning and be able to see! We blessed Him that He is *"matir asurim,"* He straightens up those who are bent over. We thank God that we are able to get up in the morning, difficult as it is, and indeed, when we think upon it, we ought to be suffused with a special light of thankfulness that we are not confined to bed, that we have the wherewithal to arise and go about our daily activities. Every word of prayer that we say, every expression of gratitude, ought to be completely new every morning. And indeed, this is true for objective reasons as well. Although the world looks like an old one, although the objects of nature are ancient and its laws timeless, nonetheless we believe that God "renews in His goodness every day the work of Creation." In that case, every morning we are indeed confronted with a brand new world – and therefore our reaction ought to be one of novelty and amazement and marveling.

The Kabbalistic tradition, as it came to us through Rabbi Isaac Luria, insisted that the same holds true for all of prayer. In prayer, perhaps above all else, we find the Jewish penchant for tradition and the acceptance of tried and tested formulae. Unlike most other peoples, especially in the Western world, our *tefillot* are the same every day, every Sabbath, every festival. And yet Rabbi Isaac Luria taught that each prayer must be unique in its essence, despite the identity of words. No two prayers are ever alike! Each prayer is offered up only once and cannot be truly repeated – provided that we pray in the right manner.

Hasidism made this the cornerstone of its whole theology. Thus, Rebbe Nachman Bratzlaver declared that, "If we shall be no better tomorrow than we are today, then why is tomorrow necessary at all?!"

We may not use the same garments of this year for next Yom Kippur. There must always be something different, for a change in the life of the spirit is necessary to keep the mind and heart alive, healthy, and alert – to make each and every tomorrow unexpected, meaningful, exciting, and hence, necessary. There must be a change – and always in an upward direction.

Paradoxically, if we remain the same, we really are diminished. If we are stationery, then we are not stationery but we retrogress. In the life of Torah, the old rule (*Sifre, Eikev* 48) holds true – "If you abandon it for one day, it will abandon you for two days." Why is this so? Because life moves on, turbulently and inexorably. Events are never static; we have to run to keep in place.

This is especially true with the *mitzva* of *tzedaka*, charity. I am often frustrated when I appeal for charitable contributions and I hear the answer to my appeal in the form of a question: "Well, what did I give last year?" In all other aspects of life, we accommodate ourselves to a precipitate change in the economy. Despite an ephemeral boycott or occasional whimper or complaint, we adjust soon enough to paying more for beef and onions, for haircuts and services. But when it comes to charity – rarely do we keep pace. "What did I give last year" becomes the introduction to and excuse for repeating the same pledge this year. This question and this pledge form a philanthropic litany which is destructive of our greatest communal institutions.

But this is not the way it should be. We may not use the same garments of this year for next Yom Kippur. Just as in matters of prayer or observance or religious experience, so in matters of charity we must grow Jewishly. Here too there must be something different for a change. Today must not be the same as yesterday, tomorrow not the same as today, this year not the same as last year.

Perhaps all that I have been saying is summed up in the last will and testament of one of the greatest Jewish translators of the Middle Ages, Rabbi Judah Ibn Tibbon, when he left the following advice to his son, Rabbi Samuel: "Of what good is life if my actions today are no different from what they were yesterday?" And conversely, how wonderful can life be if every day is new, if every day is different, if every day there is a change for the better.

Kedoshim

The Meaning of Holiness[1]

*K*edusha, holiness, is by all means the most important principle of Judaism. The highest ideal to which any person can aspire is that of holiness. All the commandments of the Torah were given so that Israel could become a *"goy kadosh,"* "a holy Nation" (Exodus 19:6). And if holiness is really this important, if it is incumbent upon every person to try for holiness – *"kedoshim tihyu,"* "thou shalt be holy," as the Bible puts it in today's portion (Leviticus 19:2) – then it is important for us to understand the meaning of holiness.

The first thing to be said about holiness is that it means something higher and nobler. Our Rabbis (*Sifra, Kedoshim* 1:2) explained *"kedoshim tihyu"* as *"perushim yihyu,"* "thou shalt be separated," above, higher. Holiness means rising above the commonplace and the vulgar, being exalted above the everyday and the secular. It means taking the soul off to a side and purifying it from the dross which it gathers in the rough and tumble of daily existence. An idea is holy when it is above

---

1. March 23, 1953.

other ideas. A human being is holy when he or she is separated from and higher than other human beings.

A corollary of this idea is that we are not to tamper with that which is holy if we are to keep it holy. A *sefer Torah* is not sacred in and of itself, but only because of what we get from it and the attitude we take towards it. No wonder therefore that Jewish law prevents us from touching the scroll with our hands. Take too free and liberal an attitude with what is sacred and it becomes profane. The first of today's portions records a commandment to the High Priest himself to keep that which is holy above everyday use and common handling – God told Moses to speak to his brother Aaron and tell him not to enter the Holy Temple whenever he so wished at any time (Leviticus 16:2). That which is holy is to be approached with reverence, it must be "*perushim*" – above, separated, and isolated.

The story is told of a young girl who had been studying at an American college and came from a wealthy home. One summer her father took her on a tour of famous European cities and came to the home where Beethoven lived and composed his great music. When the young lady noticed the piano which the guide told her was Beethoven's, she approached it with ecstasy and began playing the finest score she had learned in school. After she was finished she asked the guide, "I suppose all the greatest pianists of Europe come here to play on the piano of Beethoven." "No," said the guide, "just last week Paderewski was here and he refused to play on it, because he said that he was not worthy enough to touch Beethoven's piano."[2] Indeed that which is holy to a person must be respected and revered, and never dealt with casually. It must be kept above and be holy. If a synagogue is holy it must be entered not with boisterous good-fellowship, but with hushed reverence. If *tefillin* are holy they must not be dismissed as an extra burden, but put on with the deepest respect. What is holy must be kept aloft and from a distance – and the distance is up, not down.

Now the question is how does one attain this holiness, this state of being exalted and higher? Does it just "happen" to you? The answer

---

2. Ignacy Jan Paderewski (1860-1941) was a famous Polish pianist and composer.

is decidedly, no. You cannot just sit around, wish for it, and have it descend upon you. Our second point is that you have got to act, and act hard, in order to obtain this most cherished of all feelings.

A good illustration at this point would be a comparison of two mountains which are famous in Jewish history. They are Mount Sinai in the Sahara Desert and Mount Moriah in the middle of Jerusalem. Mount Sinai was that mountain about which the Israelites gathered and waited for three days until, in the words of the Bible, God descended upon the mountain in a pillar of fire. In a breathtakingly dramatic scene God came down upon Mount Sinai and delivered a Torah to a waiting people. The excitement was great, the atmosphere tense, and the event historic.

Such is the importance of Mount Sinai. The history of Mount Moriah revolves around Abraham and his son Isaac. Here God did not come down to give greatness to mankind. It was Abraham who was commanded to sacrifice his beloved Isaac atop this mountain, and it was a three day journey – not three days of waiting around – but a three day struggle with his conscience, three days of wrestling with himself, three days of thunderous conflicts between his mind, his heart and his soul. And Abraham came to the top of the mountain and lifted his hand ready to slaughter his son in accordance with God's wish – until the angel stopped him just in time, saying that he had proven his loyalty to God. Here God did not come down to man, but man rose up to meet God. This is the story of Mount Moriah. No wonder therefore that Mount Sinai was never holy to the Jews and today atop that mountain there is not a Temple but a Christian monastery. But Mount Moriah remains the holy center of Zion atop which there rose the *Beit HaMikdash*, the Holy Temple itself.

So holiness means a state of being higher and nobler and detached, and such holiness does not come automatically; it requires hard labor.

But the third point to consider is: Just how does one "rise" to *kedusha*? What is it that can make a man determine to work hard in order to obtain holiness? And the answer is: challenge. When the Torah tells us "*kedoshim tihyu*," it means not to be a hermit or recluse, not to escape from life; quite the contrary, to accept life as a challenge, meet it on its own grounds, face it and rise above it – not escape but involvement is the technique for attaining holiness.

Our Rabbis (Leviticus Rabba, *Kedoshim* 24:8) meant just that when they observed that in the book of Daniel, heaven is referred to only once as being possessed of *kedusha* (4:5), whereas concerning this world in the here-and-now, we are twice told to be holy: "*kedoshim tihyu*" and "*vehitkadishtem*" (Leviticus 11:44). And they explain that in heaven, where there is no Evil Urge, *kedusha* is mentioned only once, whereas on Earth, where man is faced with the challenge of the Evil Urge, the challenge of temptation and ambition and greed, *kedusha* is mentioned twice. For not only is holiness necessary to combat the Evil Urge, but the Evil Urge itself is the challenge which spurs us onto greater holiness, much as a crass stone will sharpen the blade of an expensive knife. And in order to illustrate this point, our Rabbis tell the story of a king who appointed guards for his wine-cellar – half of them *nezirim*, people who never drink alcoholic beverages, and the other half *shikorim*, chronic alcoholics. After the day's work, the king paid the *shikorim* twice as much as the *nezirim* – because it required twice the energy, twice the perseverance, and twice the will-power for the *shikorim* to resist the temptation to taste the wine.

It certainly is easy for a person of wealth and substance to observe the Sabbath. If such an individual does so, he is a good Jew – but not necessarily a holy one. But let a poor person, who would go hungry if he did not work on Shabbat, observe the Sabbath – such a person is holy. Such an individual has met the *yetzer hara* and conquered it. Such an individual has two measures of holiness, and is therefore holier than others.

This congregation knows how I feel about people who center their entire religious lives about the saying of *kadish*. And yet I cannot help but see a spark of *kedusha* in a man who has not visited a synagogue in years, or perhaps even in decades, a man who has forgotten his *Ivrit* (Hebrew) and can read only with the greatest difficulty, come to shul to recite the *kadish* despite the stares that greet his faltering recitation and perhaps the sneer and ridicule of those who are more accustomed to prayer. It is a challenge for a man of that sort to rise to the saying of *kadish* – and if he does, more power to him – twice the *kedusha*!

And this matter of accepting the challenge to holiness is not restricted to only Shabbat or *kadish*. It covers the entire world of human endeavor. In all phases of life – whether personal or communal, individual or collective – it holds true that the greater the challenge, the greater the holiness.

The simplest answer to our quest for the meaning of holiness, the one which includes our three points of being above, requiring action, and rising to challenges, lies in the entire portion we just read. Would you like to know how to be holy, "*kedoshim tihyu*"? Then read on as the Torah teaches us: Revere parents and treat them with respect; observe the Sabbath, no matter what the cost; do not worship the idols of our day, whether they be profit and money, or science and quack cures for the spirit; be charitable and philanthropic, not miserly and parsimonious; do not steal; do not be treacherous and two-faced, do not be a fence-sitter; do not lie or otherwise conceal the truth; pay your laborers on time, cut out the sweat-shops and do not exploit the less fortunate; do not put a stumbling block under the blind man; do not obstruct justice; do not slander one another and talk evil of a man behind his back; do not hate another person; and, finally, "Thou shalt love thy neighbor as thyself." All of these sound everyday-ish and ordinary. Yet holiness is their result. Meet the challenges of life in these matters and you will have risen to the ethereal heights of holiness.

Such, then, is the eminently practical meaning of holiness in Judaism. Respect it, work for it, accept it as a challenge – and it will give you that uplift which spells the difference between a life boring in its monotony and one thrilling in its adventurous elevation.

Let Criticism Be Welcome[1]

I

t may come as a surprise to some of us that criticism is not only regarded as a virtue by Judaism, but is included as a full biblical commandment, one of the 613 *mitzvot*: "Thou shalt not hate thy brother in thy heart; thou shalt surely rebuke thy neighbor, and not bear sin because of him" (Leviticus 19:17). As long as a person is rational he will form opinions about his fellow human beings; and as long as his fellow human beings are, in fact, human, they will be imperfect. It is natural, therefore, that our judgment of each other sometimes be adverse. If we cannot and do not express these criticisms, then our neighbors will never know their own faults and we shall grow to dislike them more and more – in our hearts. It is better for them and for us that we express these criticisms and articulate the rebuke – "thou shalt surely rebuke" – and thus prevent all of society from falling into sin.

Indeed, not only is criticism one of the most important commandments, but it is one of the main functions of all religion. Torah was meant to serve as the spiritual leaven in the life of man and society.

---

1. April 29, 1961.

It was meant to raise us higher and higher. This it does by serving as our critic, by focusing the spotlight of attention on the distance between the ideal and the real, by revealing to us our imperfections and thus urging us to strive for the perfect.

Moses and Balaam were both prophets. They lived at the same time and preached to the same people of Israel. Moses was incisive, merciless in his criticism of his people, and caused them great unhappiness by making them painfully aware of their inadequacy. Balaam, the gentile prophet, spoke only kind words to them. He hailed them, complimented them, blessed them, flattered them – while Moses berated them as stubborn and corrupt. And it was Balaam who greeted them with *"ma tovu,"* "How goodly are your tents, O Jacob" (Numbers 24:5). Yet it is Moses who is the archetype of the *navi ha'emet*, the true prophet, while Balaam is the *navi hasheker*, the prophet of falsehood. Moses, who criticized, is truly a prophet; Balaam, who did not, is merely a soothsayer – literally, he said soothing things calculated to put his happy listeners into moral slumber and spiritual stupor. At the time that Moses spoke our ancestors may have felt scandalized by his irritating remarks. Yet the judgment of history was reverence for the prophet and critic, and utter condemnation for the soothsayer and propagandist. Moses made of us a holy people. Balaam almost pushed us over the threshold of depraved immorality with the daughters of Moab.

What Moses was to his generation, the Torah of Moses must be to every generation, including, especially, our own. When religion begins to do nothing more than tranquilize us, soothe us, and sanctify our status quo, it is no longer religion; it is then merely a shallow therapy for arm-chair psychiatrists. It is Balaam's trademark. It is when religion fails to criticize that it deserves to be criticized itself – just as Balaam who should have criticized and did not was himself the object of criticism by his donkey.

That is why the pulpit too must be not only a source of inspiration and education, but even more so, criticism. It may occasionally be annoying, even irritating. But if our imperfections are hidden behind a veil of innocuous platitudes, then the voice of Torah has been silenced. The great Talmudic teacher Abaye once remarked (*Ketubot* 105b) that if a rabbi is very much liked by the townspeople it is often not so much because of his superiority but because of the fact that he tactfully refrains from every kind of criticism!

When we insist, time and again, that Orthodoxy today must not be silent, we do not mean merely that it avail itself of every channel of publicity just to mimic others and, so to speak, jump on the organizational bandwagon of other groups. Cooperate we must; but in all matters we must, on the basis of our Torah ideals, be critical and expose that which is non-Jewish and anti-Jewish. Whether it be a question of federal aid to Jewish day schools or a problem of synagogue architecture or a matter of kosher or non-kosher meals at the affairs of Jewish organizations, we must never be afraid to be respectfully critical. "Thou shalt surely rebuke thy neighbor." As long as we regard our fellow Jew as our "neighbor," we must not abstain from the *mitzva* of criticism.

What is true for religion is true for democracy. A democracy cannot survive if there is no right of criticism. The freedom to criticize the government is what determines whether the government is a democracy or a dictatorship. The difference between a good democracy and a poor one is the extent to which the citizens avail themselves of this right. No nation, society, or people can live on a high moral plane if criticism is either absent or suppressed. That is why we American Jews should not consider it an act of treachery when one of us is critical of the State of Israel, provided it is done in the proper spirit. Nor should we be hypersensitive to some of the very justified criticism leveled at American Jewry by our Israeli brothers. The Rabbis rightly declared (*Shabbat* 119b) that Jerusalem was destroyed because its citizens failed to exercise their duty to criticize one another.

Our Rabbis even ventured the idea that criticism has a place in domestic life. "A love which does not contain the element of criticism is not really love" (Genesis Rabba 54:3). A love between husband and wife in which there is no recognition of each other's faults is static and must soon fade away. When love is not blind but critical, when there is an attempt, in the spirit of love, to improve each other, then that love is dynamic, it leads to growth and development.

But of course this is a tall order. The practice of criticism, in the spirit the Torah means it, is a most difficult art. It is so painful to be criticized, even for small things, especially when we realize that the reproach is justified. And it is even more difficult to reprove a friend in the proper manner, so that I cause him the least anguish and am most assured that the criticism will have a successful result – the correction of the mistake. How interesting that in an age far richer in greatness and nobility than ours, the sainted Rabbi Tarphon remarked, "I wonder if there is anyone left in this generation who knows how to take criticism" – and Rabbi Alazar ben Azariah answered, "I would be more surprised to find someone left in this generation who knows how to give criticism" (*Arakhin* 16b). If my purpose in criticizing you is only that I seem bigger in comparison, that I sadistically needle you, then I am captious, not critical; then my remarks are a sin, not a *mitzva*; for then I do not observe "You shall surely rebuke," but rather commit the sin of insulting another human being (*Avot* 3:11). True criticism, said the philosopher poet Yehuda haLevi (*Kuzari* 5:20), is such that you must reprove with intent to improve – in other words, *teshuva*, repentance, or religious and moral growth, must be the goal of criticism. And this noble aim of "Thou shalt surely rebuke" can be achieved only if it is given in a spirit of profound friendship, in love, in loyalty; the object of the reproof must be "thy neighbor," your dear friend, and you must give it so that he remains your friend. The Talmud (*Sanhedrin* 101b) maintains that Jerobam, the idol-worshipping king who split Jewry into two nations, was rewarded with the crown because he had the courage to criticize King Solomon. And why was he ultimately punished? Because he reproached him publicly and thereby embarrassed him! Great is the man who can accept criticism. Greater yet is he who welcomes it. But greatest of all is he who knows how to administer it in a spirit of love and sensitivity, without causing pain and chagrin.

One last point, the most important, remains to be made. Until now we have spoken of the criticism of others. Yet this is only the prelude to the most difficult art – criticism of one's self. How does one go about reproaching himself? The great Ba'al Shem Tov taught that you arrive at self-criticism through your criticism of others. That is how he explains the well-known *mishna* (*Avot* 4:1) that "Who is wise? He who learns from every man." When you look into a mirror, the Ba'al Shem tells us, you see all your own faults and deficiencies – the shape of your nose, the complexion of your skin, the size of your teeth. So when you look at your fellow man and notice *his faults*, treat him as a mirror, and recognize in him *your own faults*. For it is a part of human nature that you see only those defects in a friend which you yourself posses to a greater or lesser degree. He who has a slight tendency to depart from the truth will be quick to detect the same characteristic in another. The same holds true for the inclination to take that which belongs to another, or immorality, or bragging, or any other vice. Our own faults sensitize us to them in others. The wise man is the person who learns from every other man – who sees his failings and then knows he has them himself and proceeds to correct them. He holds up the personality of his friend as a mirror of his own. Criticism of others, if undertaken in the Torah spirit, leads to self-criticism. Perhaps that is why the Torah uses the double verb, for greater emphasis – not only "*hokhei'aḥ*," criticism of others, but "*tokhiaḥ*," reproach of yourself. Interestingly, the word "*hokhei'aḥ*" is from the same root as the word "*viku'aḥ*," a debate or dialogue. For when I criticize my friend, even if he does not say a word, he is the mirror of my own faults, and I am automatically, through him, criticizing myself. "*Hokhei'aḥ tokhi'aḥ*" is a two-way street.

We Jews have had this quality of self-criticism in abundance. It is evident in our national sense of humor, so often turned inwards. It is evident in the writings of our prophets, who stung us with their pointed barbs. It is evident in the thorough way in which the Talmud exposes the least error of a Moses or a David. It is evident in the remarkable fact that, after having been driven out of our homeland by people no better than us – probably far worse – we say in our holiday prayers "we deserved it" – "*umipnei ḥata'einu galinu mei'artzeinu*," "and because of our sins we were exiled from our land."

"Who shall ascend the mountain of the Lord, and who shall stand in His holy place? He who has clean hands and a pure heart; who has not taken My name in vain nor sworn deceitfully. He shall receive a blessing from the Lord and righteousness from the God of his salvation" (Psalms 24:3-5).

How are hands cleaned and hearts purified? With the soap of criticism and the scouring powder of self-criticism.

How Relevant Should Halakha *Be?*[1]

Image I

t is common today to hear demands from all segments of the population that religion be made relevant to the great public issues of our time. Jews have been no less insistent than others in pressing this demand upon the teachers of Judaism. Orthodox Jews too, especially the young, ask that the *Halakha* be examined so that it yield decisive opinions on the critical problems of our day, from Vietnam to Black Panthers, from the World Court to Soviet Jewry. Rabbis are often berated for failing to pronounce on such issues in the name of *Halakha*. The Chief Rabbinate of Israel is most often criticized, especially by Western Jews, for its failure to declare the halakhic position on issues upon which other leaders of world religions have taken a stand.

It is worth studying this criticism and examining the issue as a theoretical or ideological one. Such a discussion will introduce us to a lively debate that has been going on for the past several years, mostly in Israeli journals, and the roots of which go back to differing conceptions in the early Middle Ages, even into the classical period of Judaism.

---

1. May 8, 1971.

The underlying assumption of those who press these demands might be called the "moralistic" conception of Judaism. The theory of those who advocate this approach is that Judaism is primarily a moral code, an ethic. All its laws, even those apparently remote from moral problems, can be shown to support, in the final analysis, certain ethical notions. Thus, such laws as *kashrut*, the ban on idolatry, family purity, etc., either can be made to yield ethical values – such as reverence for life, prevention of pain to animals, consideration for a wife, etc. – or they can be accepted as a form of discipline which, in its total effect upon the personality, refines us, makes us kindly, loving, charitable, righteous.

Therefore, since all of Judaism is ultimately geared to a moral value system, Judaism must have an opinion on all the great moral issues which disturb the minds of men.

At the opposite end of the spectrum is what might be called the "theocentric" conception of Judaism. Prof. Yeshayahu Leibowitz, a distinguished thinker and a maverick in the Orthodox Jewish community of Israel, is most closely identified with this position (see, for instance, his article in the winter 5731 issue of *De'ot*). His approach, which has points of similarity with the Christian thinkers Søren Kierkegaard and Karl Barth, is that religion has no monopoly on morality. Even secularists and atheists can be and often are moral individuals, without recourse to a religious foundation. The business of religion is simply God and revelation. You cannot ask of Judaism to pronounce morally on political and social and economic problems, because Judaism is not identical to ethics or morality. He does not mean to say that, Heaven forfend, Judaism is immoral; rather, there is no such separate category as ethics or morality in the world of Judaism. Judaism is *Halakha*, the way to live in this as determined by the will of God. It is a form of *avodat Hashem*, the service of the Lord. What appears as moral legislation – such as the many laws in this morning's *sidra*, including love of the neighbor, not taking revenge, not deceiving another, telling the truth, etc. – is simply the divine will as applied to social relationships. We follow these laws not because they are moral, but because they are *Halakha*, the way we serve the Lord.

The difference between morality and the *Halakha* is this: Morality assumes that man is the center of the world, and therefore all must be made to serve him. Hence the statement by Kant that man is an end in himself, that he is the source of value. But Judaism holds that man, by himself, is nothing but an advanced animal who sometimes is worse than a beast. He is vanity and the striving after wind, a cipher, a nothing.

"Man hath no preeminence above a beast, for all is vanity" (Ecclesiastes 3:19). When does man attain value? Only when he relates to God! That is the climax of the *Ne'ila* prayer on Yom Kippur: "You separated man from the beginning and recognized him as worthy of standing before You." Only when man stands before God, only when he serves his Maker, does he attain his full dignity as a human being.

For the advocates of the theocentric position, therefore, morality as such is a form of idolatry, because it misuses religion to serve man instead of God. What others call "moral" legislation is observed by us not because it is moral, but because it is God's will. Thus, to take the most blatant example, we are told, "Thou shalt love thy neighbor as thyself" (Leviticus 19:18); but the last two words that follow are more important: "*ani Hashem,*" "I am the Lord" – and that is why you must love your neighbor!

Hence, *Halakha* has no political or social program, and while we may react to issues on the basis of intuitive moral judgment, we dare not claim for them the authority of Judaism. As religious individuals, all we can do is look for religious values and religious interests in each situation and attempt to enhance them. And this depends on each individual's own honest judgment.

Actually, these two opposing interpretations – one that Judaism is morality, and the other that Judaism has no relation to morality – were anticipated or prefigured by two differing interpretations of the opening words of this week's sidra, "*kedoshim tihyu,*" "Thou shalt be holy" (Leviticus 19:2). Rashi, quoting a Tannaitic midrash, interprets those words as "Separate yourselves from sexual immorality." Holiness is defined as a deepening moral awareness and practice. Here we have the seeds of the moral conception. There are others who interpret the words "*kedoshim tihyu,*" and the concept of holiness, in a theocentric fashion. Thus, Rudolf Otto, in *The Idea of the Holy*, interprets holiness as the "numinous," the feeling of utter dread and creatureliness in the face of the infinite Lord of the Universe. God's holiness means that He is totally beyond us, utterly transcendent, that He is absolutely independent of anyone or anything or any values, including moral or ethical values. His commandments are the expression of His will, unfettered by any previous considerations that may appeal to us. It is not that God commands that which is moral, but that that which He commands becomes the right. (Many great halakhists have implicitly accepted this interpretation.)

Both views, the moralistic and the theocentric, polarize Judaism – they split the indivisible into two parts: pure religion (including revelation and *Halakha*) and ethics or morals. One school prefers one, the other prefers the other.

I believe that both of these extreme interpretations are mistaken in their failure to do justice to the comprehensive nature of Judaism.

The theocentrists err when they deny the existence of Jewish morality as such. The Torah itself often appeals to our conscience and our intuitive moral judgments. Thus, "Thou shalt do that which is right and good" (Deuteronomy 6:18), "Justice, justice shalt thou follow" (Deuteronomy 16:20) – these are not specific laws, but a general principle of morality. We are told that the other nations will envy us because of our "righteous laws and ordinances." God reveals Himself in the thirteen attributes of mercy and love. And, "The holy God is sanctified through righteousness" (Isaiah 5:16). So the moral impulse certainly is recognized by the Torah.

However, the moralists too are wrong. Even if they do not realize it, they tend to secularize religion and to use it as a *hekhsher*, a form of approval, for the simplistic morality to which they are pre-committed. More often than not, their so-called demand for relevance of *Halakha* is not a quest for guidance, but for a rubber stamp on the latest political fashions. Is it not true that most of those who demand that *Halakha* be relevant to the issues expect a particular answer on the questions of Vietnam or Civil Rights or ecology?

There is always a danger that those who identify religion with morality will sooner or later cast away those aspects of religion which are not immediately moral or didactic in nature. The casuistry with which they reinterpret non-moral material to yield moral values soon withers away and they are left only with what is immediately moral in nature. That is what happened with Christianity – the "ritual" material vanished, and they were left only with the obviously moral. That is why they maintain that the Ten Commandments are to be accepted, the rest may be ignored. It is for this reason that the Sages abandoned the custom of reading the Ten Commandments together with the *Shema* in the Temple: "They abolished the custom of reading the Ten Commandments because of the murmuring of the heretics," i.e., the heresy of the early Christians (*Berakhot* 12a). Even today I am amused when people tell me, "Rabbi, I observe only the Ten Commandments." The man who tells that to me may be a total stranger, but I am prepared to take an oath that it is not, strictly speaking, true. In order to observe the Ten Commandments, you must observe the Sabbath as well; and I have never met a Sabbath-observer who is satisfied only with the Ten Commandments...

The either/or choice between religion and morality is a form of spiritual schizophrenia. It results in a truncated Judaism which cannot survive.

What then? *Halakha* contains both moral and non-moral material. I prefer the interpretation of Nachmanides of the commandment to be holy. For him, the two words at the beginning of this morning's *sidra* are a commandment to "*kadeish atzmikha bemutar lakh*," not to take full advantage of all permissions the Torah gives us. He believes that it is possible to observe the *Halakha* strictly, and yet to be a "*naval birshut haTorah*" – observant, yet not a *mentsch*; morally degraded even while technically or conventionally observant. What he means to say is that Judaism is more than the sum of its parts – there is an integrating quality that includes and comprehends all elements that go into the make-up of Judaism.

So, Judaism contains, but is not identical to, morality. In addition to ethical material there are the elements of submission to the divine will even when we do not understand; renunciation; a sense of the mystery of God and the world; spiritual striving; and the contemplation of destiny. *Kedusha*, as today's *sidra* amply illustrates, covers the whole range of values that man can ever hope to know.

Why then does not the *Halakha* make "relevant" pronounce-
ments? My answer is based upon a certain insight into the nature of
Halakha (see the article by Prof. David Flusser in the same issue of *De'ot*
mentioned above). *Halakha* touches every area of life and offers its
judgments in an attempt to sanctify life by making man God-conscious.
However, it does not presume to cover all of life and every aspect of it.
Most of the specific decisions that you and I will make within the next
few days are neutral or indifferent to *Halakha* – the decision whether
you will take a bus or a taxi to work, what you will sell or buy, the color
suit you will wear, whether you will stroll up Central Park or Riverside
Drive, whether your children will join one youth group or another or
neither. You make hundreds of decisions every day which are not ger-
mane or of concern to the *Halakha*. This is the way it is – and this is the
way it should be.

For Jews, then, to speak in the name of *Halakha* officially on specific political or economic or social issues is wrong because, first, it is
presumptuous. There is nothing I have been able to find in the classical
Halakha or in the modern expositors of *Halakha* on Vietnam, the two-
China policy,[2] or the desirability of ping-pong as a diplomatic technique.
Second, it is dangerous. The *Halakha*, when it does pronounce, sets a
legal precedent, and legal precedents are soon invested with emotion
and tradition and become fixed, which is as it should be. However, once
we pronounce halakhically on such issues of the day, we find that the
issues change quite rapidly, and then we are caught in the dilemma of
an obsolete halakhic decision. For example, the Boers fought against
the Englishmen and they sought independence; the *Halakha* should
have supported them. But now the Boers persecute the Africans, and we
should be against the Boers. With the speed of modern life and changing
political conditions, all we can accomplish by tying *Halakha* to politics
is to entrap the *Halakha* in a hopeless maze. Third, many of the great
issues of our day are unclear. They are so enormously complex that they
defy simplistic decisions. If one wishes to hold on to a primitive morality which sees in black and white and discounts complexities as the work

---

2. The debate over whether China and Taiwan are two separate nations.

of some demon in the Pentagon, that is one's privilege. But *Halakha* cannot operate that way. Everyone agrees that we ought to have peace in the world; some think we ought to have it by rushing out of Vietnam, others by staying there to avoid a later conflagration. Everyone agrees that we ought to help Soviet Jewry; some think we can do it by protest, and others by keeping absolutely quiet and working behind the scenes. *Halakha* cannot decide on such techniques.

So Judaism, which is not only a form of morality, should not risk an official stand or *pesak Halakha* (legal decision). And rabbis and professors of religion should not assume that they are the Jewish oracles of our day.

However, since many of these issues do present moral questions, can Judaism remain indifferent as to the choice between good and evil?

No. But here the answer must come not from religion officially, but from the religious personality. The response must issue from a person as a personal decision, and one that is informed by religious experience, knowledge, and living. It must be not *din Torah*, but *da'at Torah*.

Hence, we must be careful to distinguish between cases where Judaism may have a direct judgment – such as the advisability of abortion, in most cases; exploitation of the underprivileged; euthanasia – and those where no clear judgment can be expected from *Halakha*, and where the answer must therefore come from a person with religious orientation rather than as an official religious answer, such as the problems of Vietnam or the economy.

I respect Christian clergymen and rabbis who manage to have fiery judgments and passionate opinions on every great issue of the day, whether Vietnam, Kent,[3] abortion, public aid to private schools, or Civil Rights. Sometimes I wish I could be as well-informed and as single-minded and passionate on all these issues. I respect them for their personal opinions, and I will consider them. But I challenge any

---

3. On May 4, 1970, the Ohio National Guard shot and killed nine Kent State students and injured four more. The students had been protesting the American invasion of Cambodia.

Jew to become a dogmatic spokesman for Judaism or *Halakha* on such complicated issues where *Halakha* itself, in reality, has said nothing.

To conclude, the answer must be a personal one, informed by religion, but not an institutional one.

Torah means guidance. And it is to Torah that the Jew must look for guidance. *Halakha* means a way in life, and that is the way that the Jew must seek for himself. But it is dangerous and treacherous to misuse that guidance for something for which it was not meant, and to presume to follow that way to a goal to which it does not seek to lead us. We must use extreme caution before venturing to speak authoritatively in the name of Torah or *Halakha* or Judaism.

It would do well for all of us to remember the prayer recited by Rabbi Neḥunya ben Hakanah as he entered the academy where momentous decisions awaited him (*Berakhot* 28b): "May it be Your will, O Lord my God, that no mishap occur because of me, that I not be guilty of misapplication and misleading in my decisions, and that I do not fail in any manner of *Halakha* – by rendering a wrong decision, or pretending to render a decision in its name when it is not applicable... and that my friends and colleagues do not err in their interpretation of *Halakha*. So I will be happy in them, and they will be happy with me."

Out of Respect[1]

O ne of the most memorable commandments in this *sidra* is that concerning respect for the aged: "Thou shalt rise before the hoary head (*mipnei seiva takum*) and honor the presence of the old man (*vehadarta penei zakein*), and thou shalt fear thy God; I am the Lord" (Leviticus 19:32).

Society has not done too well by this commandment. It is not easy to do so, especially in a time and country where the elderly population is increasing rapidly, creating problems in proportions unknown before. Moreover, part of the heritage left to us by the recently deceased counter-culture is an infectious stridency in which the young shout at the old as an act of political morality.

We Jews have done exceedingly well by this norm historically, but far less well, often to the point of disgrace, in our own days.

But my theme for the present is not the institutionalized aspects of *kibud zekeinim* (honor for the aged), but our personal relationships to the elderly and to the scholarly; for tradition has conventionally

---

1. April 19, 1975.

assigned to each half of this parallelism – rising before the "hoary head" and honoring the presence of the "elderly" – two different definitions, declaring the "hoary head" to refer to those who are chronologically old, and defining *"zakein"* as one who is old in wisdom even though young in years. To both categories, the elderly and the wise, we must act out of respect.

That such respect is somewhat lacking nowadays is evident from the experience of all of us. Permit me to share with you a few scenes. A few weeks ago, here at the Jewish Center, some youngsters – they were not our own youngsters – came down in an elevator filled with elderly folk. When the elevator came to the landing, the young people pushed past the elderly ones with such force, that they left the old people dazed and frightened.

Another scene, a bit less troubling but also not encouraging: Several years ago, on a Saturday afternoon, I walked into the lobby of the Jewish Center together with an elderly gentleman. Around the table were seated one adult and several youngsters, amongst them a few young people who were my students. When we walked in, the adult rose and greeted us respectfully. The youngsters merely nodded in our direction, muttered a semi-intelligible greeting which I assume was meant to be *"Gut Shabbos,"* and proceeded to act as if these two unwanted presences had accommodatingly made themselves invisible. Instead of acting out of respect, they presumably simply ran out of respect.

There is another scene that is fairly ubiquitous and which was apparently foreseen by the Sages. In their comments on two words in our verse, *"veyareita meiElokekha,"* "thou shalt fear thy God," they remark (*Sifra, Kedoshim,* 3:7) that the fulfillment of respect for the elderly requires the fear of God as well – thus, if one does not fear God he will act as if he does not see the old man or old woman approaching, and close his eyes or turn his face. But if he is truly God-fearing, he will attempt no such subterfuge, but will rise.

Is it not possible that our Rabbis were gifted with prophecy, or with at least a most remarkable prescience? That in their great wisdom they were able, so many hundreds of years ago, to foresee the behavior of young New Yorkers in their subways and trains, who read their newspapers casually – but suddenly, upon the approach of an old man or woman, will begin to study the newspaper with the care and intensity one usually reserves for a "difficult" Rambam, as normal eyesight suddenly fails and, in their near-sightedness, they bury their very noses in the paper?

Do my comments mean that I am complaining about "the younger generation"? Yes and no. Yes, because they still have a long way to go before they act out of respect without running out of respect. And no, because even the most cursory glance at history, from Scripture to our own days, will reveal that this is a perennial complaint against the younger generation! Every generation was accused of acting disrespectfully towards its elders, and it in turn leveled the same accusation at the generation that followed. Moreover, if we speak about youngsters in our own community, I believe that today's young people are no worse than youngsters were in the days when I was in my teens.

Indeed, there is some merit to the reverse. For instance, this past week there passed away an old and distinguished man of saintly personality – Rabbi Jacob Lesin, of blessed memory. In his younger years, when I went to Yeshiva, he was the *mashgiah ruhani*, the spiritual supervisor. For the last many years, until his death in his late 90's, Rabbi Lesin was inactive and therefore unknown to the overwhelming majority of Yeshiva University students. Yet they all came to his funeral and crowded into Lamport Auditorium. The funeral orations lasted well in excess of an hour and a half, and all were in Yiddish – a language almost totally unknown to 99 percent of the students. Yet, they stayed out of respect and did not leave. Surely this is a tribute to them!

Moreover, our Sages make a point of teaching that this relationship between young and old is not a one-way street. It is not a carte blanche for older people to legitimate their orneriness and impose themselves upon younger people. Rabbi Simeon ben Elazar teaches (*Kiddushin* 32b) that the commandment to honor the aged is followed by the words, "And thou shalt fear thy God," meaning that that the old man too must fear God! He must not cause unnecessary distress to the young, abusing his status by destroying the peace of mind of those who would like to observe the proprieties, and inconvenience others by unreasonably demanding respect and honor.

Yet, after all is said and done, the fact remains that respect for the old is a foundation-stone of Torah and a cornerstone of our sacred *mesora* (tradition). Our tradition teaches that the Lord Himself honors the aged. And in the Kabbala, one of the Names of God is "The Ancient of Days."

What is the rationale for this *mitzva*? It is difficult to discern. It may be an expression of concern for those weaker than we – and the aged, who feel their strength ebbing, are certainly in that category. Thus, our verse is followed by the commandment, "Thou shalt not oppress the stranger." The stranger shares with the elderly the feeling of powerlessness. However, this could not be the sole explanation for this law, for the *Halakha* includes also the healthy and the powerful elderly in the commandment to give them respect.

The explanation may be because time and experience both confer wisdom upon a person – the wisdom of living. Yet this is problematic. Even as there are young fools, are there not old people who are wanting in intelligence and wisdom? And the Torah commands us to honor the young who are wise, as well as the elderly; and the *Halakha* decides that we must accord honor as well to the old man or woman who is a boor, who is ignorant and unintelligent.

Perhaps the law is simply a tribute to longevity itself, to survival, to the accumulation of years of pain and joy and love and frustration, to the scars and wounds inflicted by time and successfully resisted.

Perhaps all of this is a remarkable expression of Judaism's love of life, its celebration of life itself, which is so deep that it awards honor to those who have warded off the Angel of Death from premature triumphs.

"*Mipnei seiva takum*" is independent of the particular old person, whether he is strong or weak, wise or ignorant. In all cases, we must act towards him or her out of respect.

In this connection permit me to commend to your attention a remarkable interpretation on our key verse by the saintly author of the *Or HaHayyim*. This great commentator breaks up the verse in two and says that the second is the result of the first. Thus, "you shall rise before the hoary head." And if you do, then "you will be honoring the presence of the old man," the well-known *zakein*, and that is Father Abraham!

Abraham was known as the *zakein*, as it is written, "And Abraham was old (*zakein*), well stricken in days" (Genesis 24:1).

Every time that we rise before an elderly person, we are in effect granting honor and showing respect for Father Abraham. Why is that so? Because, our commentator explains, the Midrash teaches that until the days of Abraham, old age was unknown as a physical phenomenon. People would grow old, very old, but their age would not show on their faces and in their bodies. They would live to 120 or 180 and then, one fine day, simply die. One could not tell from looking upon a man or a woman whether that person was old or young. It was Abraham who prayed to God for *seiva* (the hoary head), the signs of age, so that people might distinguish the father (Abraham) from the son (Isaac). Since it is Abraham who is responsible for the "hoary head," then whoever honors the hoary head in effect honors Abraham.

However, we are permitted to wonder: Why was Abraham so concerned with the external signs of age? Indeed, how many parents today pray for the exact reverse, striving with all their might and main to look as young as their own children? Are there not whole industries dedicated to the fulfillment of such pious prayers?

I suggest that this prayer by Abraham is a reflection of his profound humility and his admiration for his own son.

The great event in the life of both Abraham and his son Isaac, the one that was to bind them together for all of time, is the *Akeida*, the offering up of Isaac by Abraham at the command of the Lord. Throughout our liturgy, we always refer to the *Akeida* as an expression of the heroism of Abraham, of his utter devotion, of his unquestioning faith. Yet Abraham thought that the *Akeida* was a tribute not so much to him as to his son, to the unflinching courage, the consummate devotion, the magnificent submissiveness of Isaac to the word of God.

Thus, Abraham thought: If respect is to be accorded on the basis of merit, then it is I who must respect him, not he who is to honor me! If honor is conditional, and is to be given only on the basis of worth and achievement, then it is possible for a person to grow old and even ancient and never attain the least bit of dignity that comes with acknowledgement and respect by society. If only merit is to be acknowledged, what happens to the non-achiever, to the failure, to the unlucky one? Is he never in his life to achieve any recognition at all? For that matter, do parents too have to prove their worth before their children fulfill the commandment, "Honor thy father and thy mother?"

Hence, Abraham prayed for *seiva*, so that he and other "unworthy" elderly would have at least some sign – if nothing more than a white head, a furrowed brow, a wrinkled face, a stooped posture – to earn for them some token of respect and acknowledgement by the world about them, though it be formal and unrelated to merit or attainment.

Therefore, we show courtesy to a *zakein*, even if he is empty and has accomplished nothing and is ornery; we force ourselves to act with filial respect to our fathers and mothers even if we dislike them and are filled with resentment. If we do these things, we are fulfilling "*vehadarta penei zakein*," we are honoring the presence of that "old man" Abraham, indicating that he is still alive with us. We are honoring Judaism, the faith of Abraham, because we are following his teaching in rising before "the hoary head," even if we think that the hoary head crowns a body and a personality that possess no innate merit and no inherent claim to honor. We owe respect not only to those who are achievers and wise and contributors and good people, but also to the *seiva* for his own sake. That is our tribute to the *zakein* of our people and his teaching.

I therefore urge that this commandment not be neglected, but that we make special new efforts to enforce it properly. If anyone above the age of seventy (the halakhic definition of *seiva*) passes within six feet, stand up before him or her, whether Jew or gentile! If a *talmid ḥakham* (a scholar) passes by, no matter what his age – rise in his presence! The Talmud (*Makkot* 22b) refers to those who rise before the *sefer Torah* but fail to rise before the scholar who embodies and incorporates the knowledge of the *sefer Torah*, as "fools."

Indeed, I heard of a beautiful custom (which I believe is practiced by Sephardi Jews) that when a father receives an *aliya* and is called to the Torah, his children will remain standing during that entire period that he is at the Torah. I have adopted that custom in my family. When I receive an *aliya*, my children stand. When my father receives an *aliya*, I rise for that entire period. I would like this practice to be adopted by all families that constitute our Jewish Center family.

Perhaps it is best to conclude with an interpretation by Ibn Ezra who offers a reason or motivation for our law that is less worthy than the others that I mentioned, but is more compelling because it appeals to self-interest. He too refers to the end of that verse: "Thou shalt fear thy God, I am the Lord." "I am the Lord" who will still be here when you are an old man and have attained your "hoary head." When you are weak and lonely and aged, you too will pine for some bit of recognition, some token of respect. But if now, when you are young and strong, you neglect the elderly, you do not "fear thy God," then you must expect the same treatment in your own old age. Then you will indeed have something to fear! Here, then, is a religiously inspired social contract: Honor the old man now, so that you will be honored when you reach his age.

As individuals and as a community, our task is to create both the institutional forms and the patterns of personal relationships, so that the entry into *zikna* (old age) will not occasion *yira* (fear) – the fear of neglect and solitude and powerlessness – but that old age will be a period of dignity and joy; that the autumn of life will not be one of dread of the winter that follows, its coldness and barrenness, its futility and frost and forlornness, but rather will be an Indian summer of harvest and honor, in affectionate companionship with those in the spring and the summer of their lives, all under the blessed providence of the One who overarches all seasons and all ages – "I am the Lord."

Emor

The Pursuit of Fun[1]

When the Founding Fathers of America wrote the *Declaration of Independence*, they included one new phrase which was to have wide repercussions later in the history of this country. That phrase is, "the pursuit of happiness."

The idea of happiness is, of course nothing new. Americans did not invent it. It has been known in a hundred languages and experienced universally for millennia. Our own Torah dedicates three entire sections as *parashot mo'adim*, the description of the major holidays on which we are commanded, "You shall be happy in your festivals" (Deuteronomy 16:14). What was new in the formulation of the Founding Fathers was the emphasis on happiness as something to pursue.

Serious thinkers have not always looked with favor on this phrase. Not that there is anything wrong with being happy – their outlook is not jaundiced – but they have two reservations: first, is happiness really to be the highest goal of mankind? Is it subordinate to or more important than, say, the idea of duty, or respect for others, or faithfulness, or

---

honor? And second, can happiness really be acquired by pursuing it? Is it not really a rather elusive prize which you can win only indirectly by living in a certain way, and not by a direct chase?

But all these debates are really academic. Today we accept happiness as terribly important; for many it is the highest value that life has to offer. And we no longer ask questions about the wisdom of pursuing it in order to attain it. We do not simply pursue it; we are relentless, fanatic, single-minded in our hot chase of happiness. Also, we have changed the word "happiness" to "fun," and with it has come a change of the content of our aspirations. Happiness, at least, implies an ordered, harmonious way of life which offers deep satisfactions. Fun is nothing of the sort. It is escape, pure and simple. It is a matter of losing yourself consciously in a world where all tensions are released and inhibitions loosened. And the pursuit of fun has become America's chief avocation. In essence, there is nothing wrong with occasionally having fun, provided it is decent, clean, controlled, and harmless. There is no *mitzva* to be a humorless bore. Some diversion or escape is always necessary and welcome. My concern is, however, with that great number of Americans – and American Jews – who have unconsciously transformed fun from entertainment to *weltanschauung*, from casual distraction to consuming passion, from occasional release to total immersion in escape from the challenges to which life summons us. Perhaps life in this complicated, dangerous world is too deadly serious for most people – but that is an explanation, not an excuse for avoiding its problems.

Consider how the original concept of "the pursuit of happiness" has degenerated into the "fun for all" disease that affects every part of our society. At Cape Canaveral not long ago a human being was shot into space. Fortunately he returned safely – God was good to him, his wife and children, and the prestige of his country. The days and hours before the firing were tense ones. They should have been, as they were for many, a time for prayer, and the sobriety that comes from knowing that a man's life is at stake. Yet one reporter told of the carryings-on at the entertainment spots surrounding the missile area – large crowds overflowing, drinking, joking, and dancing in anticipation of the firing. Commander Shepard hovers between immortality and eternity – and Cape Canaveral turns into a carnival. A man faces the terrible loneliness of outer space, and his fellow men clutter up whatever inner space they possess with the kind of inconsiderate nonsense which degrades their stature as humans.

Here is a second example. A certain Jew who lives in the South has made a great success as a humorist by drawing upon immigrant Jewish experience in the Lower East Side.[2] He has painted funny verbal pictures with *Only in America*, and admonished us to *Enjoy, Enjoy* (another title of one of his books). Some of us may like this brand of humor, others may not. That is irrelevant. But what does one say in response to a supposedly funny piece in which he writes a kindly, good-humored description of a Jewish girl taking her vows as a Roman Catholic nun? When a prominent Yiddish writer took him to task for it, Harry Golden insulted his critic and replied that he takes such conversions in stride – with gentility, kindliness, and a sense of humor! Is this not carrying the idolatry of fun a bit too far? Jews know that on occasions of this sort you tear *keri'a* and sit *shiva* – and the apostle of good humor has fun!

The word "fun," according to Webster, comes from the Middle English *fonnen*, which means: to be foolish, to fool someone. Too much concentration on "having fun" is indeed the epitome of foolishness. And if you spend your life in that nervous, anxious, guilt-laden pursuit of fun, then you fool no one but yourself. No, this is not happiness. And it certainly is not *simḥa*.

I recently chanced upon something known as *Chase's Calendar of Annual Events*, which is a compendium of eight hundred occasions of celebration, fun, and festivity observed in the United States. We are, a reading of this book reveals, a holiday-ridden people. There is scarcely a single day in the year when some citizens in some part of this great country will not be celebrating something or other. We have every conceivable kind of holiday, from weeks dedicated to the peanut and girl scouts to months celebrating children's art, and the egg, to days hailing mothers, fathers-in-law, buzzards, and bachelors. For everything there is a parade and the occasion for some group just "to have fun." Amazing – a complete *lu'aḥ* dedicated to the principle that every day is a time

---

2. Harry Lewis Golden, an American Jewish writer and newspaper publisher.

for fun! And yet, no one will disagree, there is not a day that passes but what more and more people become more and more miserable. Fun, is evidently, a failure.

Our own Jewish calendar is one that presents us with a number of holidays and festivals. They are days of happiness, of *simḥa*. Do our holidays bear any resemblance to the fun-fare that we have been describing? Assuredly not – yet sometimes it seems that we have so assimilated to the fun-culture of contemporary America that we have failed to appreciate the vast abyss that separates them. That is why only a few years ago one of our "defense organizations" published a book purporting to acquaint our non-Jewish neighbors with the essentials of Jewish belief and practice. Although a fairly good book, a remarkable picture emerges from it: Jewish life is a merry-go-round of joy upon joy, a breathless round of celebrations, all smiling faces and wine-drinking and feasting. Rosh HaShana and Yom Kippur are primarily happy times filed with laughter and fun. Even Tisha BeAv "has lost much of its tragic overtones." The Jews, we are told, "are overjoyed that freedom is flourishing in so many parts of the world." Of course, the remnants of Eichmann's victims and the Jews in Morocco and behind the Iron Curtain are not aware of this – but then, they do not appreciate that the Jewish calendar is like the American calendar, and that both are dedicated to the proposition that the pursuit of fun is the noblest goal of man created in the image of God.

Real *simḥa* is, of course, nothing of the sort. True joy, in the Jewish sense, is not an escape from life but an intensification of its loftiest features. *Simḥa* is the elation of mankind, the elevation of our souls that comes with the realization that we stand in the presence of God – that we are not alone on the face of the earth. That is why *simḥa* is the special characteristic of the three pilgrim festivals, the *shalosh regalim*, for then the Israelite would ascend to the Temple to "be seen before the Lord" (Deuteronomy 16:16). To enjoy the companionship of God and His gifts, that is the gist of happiness. *Simḥa* does not come from avoiding the knowledge that there is evil in the world, from blinding oneself to the enormous threats of pain and death. It comes from an appreciation that in this kind of world, despite evil and sickness and pain, there *is* a God who watches over us, that we *do* have the opportunity to vanquish evil, that there *is* a vibrant, active principle of holiness and purity and goodness. We do not use the historical origin of our holidays as an excuse just to pursue happiness or have fun. The holidays are themselves expressions of joy when man faces the world with open eyes and an open heart, and each holiday has its own character and its own joyousness.

It would be too much to try to exhaust the meaning of each of the *yamim tovim*. A Jewish holiday is like a human personality – it has a thousand different facets, each more intriguing and fascinating than the next. Let us, rather, examine only one facet of each as a source of *simḥa*, as interpreted by the Hasidic sage and saint, the author of *Sefat Emet*. He points out that in Leviticus the section detailing the holidays follows immediately after the *mitzva* of *kiddush Hashem*, the sanctification of God's Name. "And I shall be sanctified amongst the Children of Israel" was interpreted by our Rabbis (*Sanhedrin* 74a) to mean that a Jew must submit to martyrdom rather than violate any of the three major sins known to Judaism – idolatry, unchastity, and murder. The three major festivals of Pesaḥ, Shavuot, and Sukkot, the *Sefat Emet* maintains, come to preserve and enhance each of these three principles for which we must be ready to give our lives in *kiddush Hashem*.

A person must give one's life if ordered to take the life of another, for homicide is an unforgivable sin. The positive principle is celebrated in Pesaḥ when we recall that God took us out of the land of slaves where life was cheap and man worthless, where babies were tossed into the Nile. Pesaḥ fills us with joy as we appreciate the transcendent value of life in a world where people usually speak of the destruction of millions of people in the impersonal terms of cold statistics. We do not just "have fun" – we are instead suffused with happiness that life was granted to us, and that we were entrusted with its safe-keeping.

The principles of morality or chastity may not be violated even under pain of death, for so is God made holy in Israel. And the festival of Sukkot reaffirms that concept of emphasizing the importance of the home. For an immoral act is in essence an offense against the family. In the presence of immorality husband and wife can have no love for each other and children and parents at worst do not know each other, and at best despise each other. Sukkot is the time we remember how our God took us out of Egypt with its lust and fleshpots, its incest, its sexual degeneracy, and led us through the desert in order that for forty years we learn to dwell in Sukkot, each family protecting the wholeness of its home and its sacred integrity. On Sukkot we are joyous that every Jewish family can hold aloft the banner of *tzeni'ut* (modesty), that we can learn to respect the personality of another human being and not treat another as merely an animate object of our desire. We are happy that we can preserve the family and home even in a world filled with *gilui arayot* (illicit relations), a world where obscenity more and more becomes legally accepted and morally respected, where degeneracy receives the sanction of literature and the blessing of art, and where home after home falls apart.

Finally, and perhaps most important, a Jew must perform *kiddush Hashem* and relinquish life itself rather than submit to idolatry. Shavuot, which commemorates the giving of Torah at Sinai, affirms the Jewish appreciation of divinity itself. We are happy that in a civilization which has silenced the voice of God by denying that He is concerned with mankind, and set up the idols of money and science instead, we Jews are the recipients of His Torah and can to this day partake in the supernatural experience of revelation by studying the Torah. When we study the Torah we know that God is not silent, that He speaks through its pages, that He has let us know how to live without loneliness, without despair, without emptiness. What a source of joy!

Here, then, is an example of how Jewish joy differs from secular "fun," of how the Jewish calendar, based upon *simḥa*, is different from the ordinary calendar. Unlike fun, which is a form of escape by being blind to life's dangers and evils, Judaism's holidays provide *simḥa* by a direct confrontation with them. Unlike fun, which is amoral, and often immoral, *simḥa* is eminently moral and ethical and spiritual. It shows you the face of a murder-bent world and tells you to revere life – the ethics of *simḥa*. It reveals to you a society corrupt with unchastity and commands you to respect the integrity of every home and family – the morality of *simḥa*. It bares before you a civilization that has forgotten God and reminds you of His ever-loving presence – the spirituality of *simḥa*.

As we say every morning in our *Shaḥarit* prayers: *"Ashreinu, ma tov ḥelkeinu,"* "Happy are we! For how good is our destiny, how pleasant our lot, how beautiful our heritage!"

The Kohen *Today*[1]

In an important essay published not too long ago, Dr. Samuel Belkin, President of Yeshiva University, presented a creative insight into the understanding of the commandments of the Torah. There is a great literature on *ta'amei hamitzvot,* the reasons for the commandments. What Dr. Belkin proposed is a fundamental distinction between the "reason" for a *mitzva* and the "purpose" of the commandment. The reason is historical, it is something about which man may speculate and conjecture; but ultimately it is known with certainty only to God Himself. Actually, the reason for legislating a *mitzva* does not make too much difference – it is of little consequence to us. What is of importance, however, is the purpose of the *mitzva.* Here we must always ask ourselves: What is it the Torah wants me to accomplish as a result of performing this *mitzva*? The reason for a *mitzva* remains the same through all eternity, although it may always remain unknown to man. The purpose may change from generation to generation, from culture to culture, from society to society. While the reason is divine, the purpose is human – and, therefore, while

---

1. May 12, 1962.

all of us observe the same *mitzvot* in the same manner, each observance may mean something subtly different for each individual person. Hence, while it may be fruitless to inquire into the reason for a *mitzva*, it is most worthwhile to investigate the purpose of the *mitzvot*.

It is in this spirit that we may ask a fundamental question about the teachings of this morning's *sidra*. That is, what is the purpose of the institution of *kehuna*, the hereditary priesthood, for modern Jews living in a free and democratic society? Centuries ago, in the days of the Temple, the priest was a most important functionary in the religious life of the country. It was he who officiated at the sacrificial rites in the Temple. He was supported by an elaborate system of tithes and so forth. Today, the *kohanim*, descendants of Aaron, the brother of Moses, are distinguished from other Jews by only a few laws, such as: they are honored with the reading of the first portion of the Torah, they may not defile themselves by contact with the dead, they are limited in their choice of a mate by certain marital regulations, and they officiate at the blessing of the congregation on the holidays. Now, in what manner can this residual priesthood be relevant to our lives and times? Once again, we do not ask for the reason, we do not demand that the Torah justify its claim upon us. We shall observe whether our limited intellectual faculties fully understand or not. But what specific purposes, what special nuances of meaningfulness lie within this biblical legislation?

There are many answers. Those that we shall mention this morning are culled especially from the commentary on the prayer book, *Olat Re'iyah*, by the late Chief Rabbi of the Holy Land, Rabbi Abraham Isaac Kook.

At the very beginning, we must understand that *kehuna* in Jewish life was never meant as a ministry of magic. The *kohen* never waved a wand or performed miracles. Rather, as we discover from a reading of the Bible, the priesthood, with all its hierarchical and hereditary features, was intimately connected with the concept of teaching, especially Torah. Thus, Ezekiel, in this morning's *haftara*, defines the function of the *kohen* as, "And they shall teach My people to distinguish between the sacred and the profane" (44:23). Malachi proclaimed, "And the lips of the priest shall keep knowledge, they shall seek Torah from his mouth" (2:7). In assigning *kehuna* to the tribe of Levi, Moses declared,

"They shall teach Your laws to Jacob and Your Torah to Israel" (Deuteronomy 33:10). *Kehuna*, therefore, is a ministry of *hora'a*, of teaching, of education and edification.

An important aspect of our daily morning service thereby becomes more significant. At the very beginning of the service, one of the first things we recite is the *birkhot haTorah*, the blessings over the study of Torah. After we thank God for giving us the Torah, we immediately proceed to perform the *mitzva* – we study Torah. And what passage of the Bible is it that we choose to recite as part of the study of Torah? The *birkat kohanim*, the blessing that is recited by the priests, "The Lord should bless you and keep you."

Why, of all the sublime passages in the Torah, do we choose the priestly blessing as the one over which to thank God for Torah? Obviously it must be because of the fact that the priests themselves are teachers of Torah or, indirectly, by their very presence in our midst they remind us and challenge us to study the Torah of the Lord.

The great medieval Spanish rabbi Abudarham observed that the priestly blessing consists of three verses. The first verse, "The Lord should bless you and keep you," contains three Hebrew words. The second verse contains five words, and the third – seven words. Abudarham remarks that the *birkat kohanim* is thus equivalent to the reading of the Torah, for on weekdays we have three *aliyot*, on holidays five *aliyot*, and on Saturdays a minimum of seven.

Rav Kook, however, goes beyond a mere arithmetical equivalence and finds deep significance in this relationship of *birkat kohanim* to *birkhot haTorah*, of priesthood to the teaching of Torah. *Kehuna*, after all, is not an anachronism. It indicates to us that there are amongst us Jews a family, descended from Aaron, who possess, as Rav Kook calls it, a *"segula kelalit haba'a biyerusha,"* a general talent or predisposition that is bequeathed by heredity. From the very earliest days of the history of our people until today, the *kehuna* has come down from father to son – a whole family, throughout all these many centuries, has been distinguished by a mandate from the Almighty that its sons be the Ministers of God in the midst of Israel, that they be charged with the function of *hora'a*, of teaching the Children of Israel, so that "they shall seek Torah from his mouth." Now the very presence amongst us of this family who is marked by these characteristics reminds us that all of us Jews, non-*kohanim* as well as *kohanim*, possess a more general and precious *segula kelalit haba'a biyerusha*, a heritage of inclination for the study of Torah. God not only gave us a Torah from above, but implanted within us a readiness to love it and a willingness to obey and follow it. There is in every Jew, by virtue of his being a Jew, this element of spirituality. Every Jew wears the crown of Torah, even as the descendants of Aaron wear the crown of priesthood.

This does not mean that every Jew is born a full-fledged lover of Torah, a mature spiritual personality – by no means. Rather, it means that each Jew has within himself the potential for these lofty ends, that if the effort is put in, he can attain them, for they are part and parcel of the national cultural heritage of our people.

Here too Rav Kook offers a comment of great insight. When the *kohanim* bless the congregation, they accompany their verbal blessing with *nesi'at kapayim*, the raising of their hands with fingers extended. To Rav Kook this is a profound symbol. It is a pointing to the future, an aspiration for transcendence, a reaching out for what is beyond, a stretching of the self to greater heights. Rav Kook reminds us that the rights and the privileges of the *kohen* to bless his fellow Israelites derive not from his own actual religious excellence, for not every *kohen* who blesses the congregation is necessarily a holy man. Rather, it derives from the charge placed upon him to be holy. Because the *kohen* is expected by the Torah to attain a greater measure of sanctity, because he was given the hereditary injunction to reach higher than others, because he was endowed with the predisposition for a great spiritual gestalt, therefore the *mitzva* of blessing the congregation devolves upon the *kohen*. The prerogative of blessing derives not from the actuality but from the potentiality of the *kohen* – not from his religious character at the present, but from that which he could attain were he to strive for it with sufficient effort and exertion. That is why the *kohen* raises his hand in the *nesi'at kapayim* – he is pointing to the future, to the realization of the potential within him. His extended arms are a bridge, which he is bidden to cross, from promise to fulfillment, from small beginnings to great achievements, from what he is to what he can and ought to be.

And this is true of all Jews with regard to Torah. At the foot of Sinai, when we were given the Torah, we were designated *mamlekhet kohanim* – a kingdom in which all citizens are priests. We are *kohanim* of Torah to all of mankind. Hence, we are different from others not because of what we are, but because of what we can and ought to be. Religious life in Judaism is not a matter only of being holy, but of becoming holier. The hands of the *kohen* raised in benediction are for every Jew the symbol of the study of Torah – constant progress, unceasing intellectual ferment, never-ending spiritual development. The *kohen* in our midst teaches us something about our own character and what we ought to do with it. He tells us, as Yehuda haLevi taught in the *Kuzari*, that Israel is caught up in the "*inyan Eloki*," marked with the indelible traces of the encounter with God. He reminds us, as the great founder of the Habad School of Hasidism taught in his *Tanya*, that every Jew is born with a "*nefesh haElokit*," with a divine soul, which contains within it an "*ahava tivit*" or "*ahava mesuteret*," a natural love for God and Torah which is hidden and unaroused. Just as a descendant of Aaron is naturally a *kohen*, a status from which he cannot resign at will, so is every Jew by nature a *homo religiosis*, a spiritual creature. Whether he knows it or not – indeed, whether he wants it or not – every Jew has a religious potential within him, the seed of spirituality, the embryo of *kedusha*. But from the *kohen* each Jew must learn that blessing can come only when, as the extended fingers symbolize, he is willing to actualize his potential, make the seed grow, develop one's embryonic talent, express one's hidden, natural resources of Torah.

So the hereditary *kehuna* certainly does have a relevant purpose for our lives. It teaches us that Judaism was not superimposed upon Jews. Rather, it is natural and preexistent in the Jewish soul. Torah may have been given from Heaven, but the receptivity of it already existed in the Jewish heart. All that Jews need to do in order to achieve blessing, for themselves and for all mankind, is to arouse and express the spirituality which lies dormant within.

It is for that reason that we loyal Jews ought to accept with great skepticism and with a sense of humor the predictions of many of our secular and non-observant co-religionists who periodically produce from amongst themselves modern *nevi'ei sheker*, false prophets, who proclaim the end of classical, traditional Judaism in Jewish life. For us it is unthinkable to imagine Jews without Judaism. Even if Torah should be forgotten for a century, it must return to its former eminence amongst Jews, for there is in us what Rav Kook called, "*segula kelalit haba'a biyerusha*," a hereditary predisposition for the spirituality of Torah; or, as the author of the *Tanya* called it, "*ahava tivit*," a natural love hidden in the divine soul in every Jew; or, as haLevi termed it, the "*inyan Eloki*." When we see before our eyes a *kohen*, a direct descendant of Aaron, the first High Priest, when we behold the physical continuity of ancient Israel and its survival into modern times, then we are seized with a great optimism and hope for the survival and ultimate triumph of the spiritual character of Israel in the future.

This is an exhilarating thought, for it encourages us never to despair of any single Jew. Within every Jewish bosom, every Jewish heart, there lies this latent love, this silent passion, this unconscious aspiration. Our sacred duty is to bring it out into the open, activate it and actualize it, to make this love conscious, so that all Israel will return to God and bring with them all of mankind.

In the words of David (Psalms 119:48), "I shall raise my hands unto Your commandments which I love, and I shall dwell upon Your laws." When we shall accept the symbol of the priestly blessing, the raising of the hands and the pointing to the future, the transition from potential to real, when we shall take that love for the *mitzvot* and actualize it by raising our hands – then we, and all Israel, will dwell upon the laws of God and become, once again, a glorious people of Torah.

So Help Me God[1]

Our *sidra* of this morning opens with the commandment to the *kohen* that he not defile himself by contact with the corpse of any person save his closest relatives. These include his father, mother, son, daughter, brother, and unmarried sister. Before these, however, appears one category which presents a problem. The Torah expresses this as *"she'eiro hakarov eilav,"* which most English translations render as, "his kin who is nearest to him" (Leviticus 21:2). This would indicate that this expression is but an introduction to the detailed list of relatives that follows. However, our tradition (*Yevamot* 22b) has declared that the word *"she'eir"* refers to one's wife who, therefore, is the first instance of a relative to whom a *kohen* may, indeed must, defile himself in order to accord her her last honor.

The question is: Why did the Torah not say directly and explicitly that the *kohen* may defile himself for his wife? Why this peculiar idiom? And if indeed *"she'eir"* does mean a wife, why is it in the masculine form?

---

1. May 13, 1967.

143

The answer offered by the *Keli Yakar* – and anticipated by the Rashbam in his commentary to the Talmud – is rather prosaic; in fact, so prosaic as to be almost banal. Yet, it says something to us of great significance. "*She'eir*" means a wife because, he tells us, the word originally means "food," as in the Biblical expression "*she'eira kesuta ve'onata*" (Exodus 21:10).

But why does the Torah use the word "*she'eir*" for "wife," when it means "food"? And the answer that is offered is: because it is she who prepares her husband's food for him!

What a disappointing and pedestrian answer! But what he means is clearly more than the reduction of the role of the wife to chief cook and bottle washer. On the contrary, the reference to a man's "*she'eir*," his wife, as "*hakarov eilav*," as one who is close to him, indicates that the wife's occupation as "*she'eir*" somehow attains a significance that makes her exceedingly close to her husband, closer than any two beings can otherwise be to each other.

In support of his answer, the *Keli Yakar* quotes a remarkable passage in the Talmud (*Yevamot* 63a) in which we are told that Rabbi Jose met (in a mystical vision) the prophet Elijah. Rabbi Jose presented to the prophet some of the problems that were bothering him. He said to the prophet: In the Torah it is written "*e'eseh lo eizer kenegdo*," that God, noticing the loneliness of Adam, said, "I shall make for him a helpmeet for him" (Genesis 2:18). Now, in what way is a wife a help for her husband? (A strange question, but a question nonetheless.) To this the prophet answered: When the husband comes home from the field and brings with him wheat, can he eat the wheat as it is? Does he not require the service of his wife in threshing it, grinding it, baking it, and thus making it fit and palatable for him? Or, he comes home laden with flax. Is it possible for him to wear the flax as it is, without his wife weaving it into a proper garment for him? By means of her assistance, she "brings light to his eyes and puts him on his feet." Thus, the function of a wife, in the material sense, is to take the raw material provided for her by her husband and make it palatable and usable for him and her family.

One wonders – for such an interpretation of the function of a wife we need the prophet Elijah? But if we look a bit deeper, we find that we have here indeed an insight of rare wisdom. For, in order to truly be one who enlightens the eyes and places a man on his feet in stability, a wife must take not only the raw material that her husband gives her, but the raw material that her husband is, and transform every great potential within him, every advantageous possibility that he possesses, into a creative reality. That is why the wife is called "*she'eir.*" For just as nutritionally she converts the wheat into bread, just as her fingers weave the flax into clothing, so psychologically she must draw out all hidden talents from her husband, she must bring out the best in him. When she has done that, in this larger sense, then indeed she is one who "brings light to his eyes and puts him on his feet."

This, then, is the true meaning of *eizer*, a helpmeet. One who "brings light to his eyes and puts him on his feet" is not a servant, or an assistant, or simply an extra pair of hands. Rather, such a woman is a catalyst of human development and progress, one who can creatively elicit from the deepest resources of a person that which is valuable, constructive, and enduring. Such an individual is an artist whose medium is the human personality, one who helps to release untapped human energy or, in the language of the Kabbala, an agent of the emergence "*min hane'elam el hagalui,*" of that which is hidden to that which is revealed.

Hence, the true wife is the kind of *she'eir* who is "*hakarov eilav,*" who is indeed close to her husband, closer than words can describe, because she is a veritable "*eizer kenegdo,*" a helpmeet for him. Just as she takes the raw food and transforms it into a palatable delicacy, so she is even closer in that she takes the raw potentialities that he brings to her – and no living, dynamic human being is ever complete and perfect – and encourages the emergence of his underdeveloped abilities. And this dynamic works both ways – in a marriage, each partner is a *she'er* for the other, bringing out the best in the other.

The same even holds true, although perhaps to a lesser extent, for any devoted relative or teacher or friend – not the least of which is a parent. The role of such a person, no matter what the relationship, is to teach not in the sense of informing, but in the sense of molding and shaping and directing the inner life so that it emerges more developed and more finely oriented.

What is true for individuals holds true for communities as well. Thus, the relationship of Israel to the United States is, or ought to be, that of husband and wife, that of one who "brings light to his eyes and puts him on his feet." On this Sabbath before Israel's Independence Day, we of course are concerned about Israel's military security and economic well-being. But over and beyond that, each country must help bring out the best in the other – each must assist the other in focalizing its major concerns and directing its energies creatively instead of squandering them diffusely. Israel must help American Jewry survive with its moral concern for other Jewries intact, and not to imagine that it is sufficient to be complete Americans of Jewish persuasion. And American Jewry must help Israel realize the purpose of its existence, which is much more than being just another Levantine state, by placing demands on its spiritual reservoirs and demanding a certain quality of life therein.

As in marriage, this creative agency of helping to bring out the best is usually through sweet reasonableness and encouragement; but sometimes, it works also through criticism and reproach and rebuke. Sometimes indeed the best way to be an *eizer* is by being *kenegdo*, over against a mate; so each of us – Israeli and American Jewry – must not be hypersensitive to criticism. It is quite alright to be *kenegdo*, provided the purpose is always to be an *eizer*. Only thus can we be for each other one who "brings light to his eyes and puts him on his feet," enlightening and stabilizing.

But most of all the greatest *eizer* is God Himself. Thus we read in the Psalms (121:1) words which are known to us through the prayer book, "*shir lama'alot*, a song of ascent, I lift up my eyes to the hills (*el heharim*), from where shall my help come? My help comes from the Lord who makes heaven and earth." The greatest *eizer* is God Himself.

Our Rabbis in the midrash on this psalm (*Yalkut Shimoni*, Psalms 879) pointed out that unlike the other psalms in this section, this one is introduced by the words "*shir lama'alot*" rather than "*shir hama'alot*," "this is a song for the purpose of steps" – that is, this song is that which assists the righteous man in rising up the steps from his own soul to the divine Throne of Glory. This psalm tells us how to bring out the best in ourselves, ascending the ladder of the spirit.

God, Torah, and faith provide for us a sense of purposefulness which enables us to harness all our energy towards one goal, like a magnet acting on a disoriented group of iron molecules, focusing all of them in one direction – or like a laser beam, which, by causing all the light rays to go in one direction, gives us a tool of unprecedented power.

Moreover, the midrash saw in this psalm about *eizer* a historical reference of great tenderness and pathos. They say that it was uttered for the first time by our father Jacob, and the word should be read not "*harim*" but "*horim*," not mountains, but parents. When Jacob was about to meet his beloved Rachel, he thought of the time that his father first met his mother. "I lift up my eyes *el heharim* (or *horim*)" means, I lift up my eyes and recall the time that my parents first met. How different were their circumstances! When they met, Isaac had Eliezer as his servant or ambassador bearing carloads of gifts and jewels and gems for his wife Rebecca. They began life with all the economic advantages that any young couple could ever want. And here I am, coming to my beloved Rachel as a fugitive from a hateful brother, fleeing for my life, in tatters, hungry and tired with not a penny to my name. "From where shall my help come?"

And his answer came: My help, my "*she'eir*," comes from the Lord, "who makes heaven and earth." God, who fashioned and ordered the world out of the primordial chaos, the "*tohu vavohu*," He will do the same for my own life. It is He who will be my *eizer* by bringing out the best in me and allowing this best to emerge from the depths of my heart and soul to overcome my infirmities and my poverty and the harshness of life about me. Indeed, Isaac and Rebecca started out life with a great deal of wealth – yet they were not altogether happy. Somehow their relationship was not quite smooth – they often failed to communicate with each other. Whereas Jacob and Rachel, despite the difficulties that beset them in the beginning, despite the harshness of their few years together and the tragedy which brought early death to Rachel, managed to attain a life which was blessed with love and affection. The quality of their relationship was sublime – many decades after her death, Jacob was to remember with warm affection the immortal bonds that held them together. No doubt the quality of their relationship was largely the result of the fact that they had to struggle during their early years, that he had to work seven years and seven years again in order to win the hand of his beloved wife, and that in this mutual struggle together each was an *eizer* for the other, each one brought out the best in the other.

This too was the way in which God proved to be an *eizer* to Jacob. He taught Jacob how to bring out the best in himself and in his wife. Indeed, the greatest gift from God is not outright blessing, but an indirect blessing in which God teaches us how to approach the raw material of life and fashion something of enduring value. We read "*ezri mei'im Hashem*," "My help is [literally] from *with* the Lord," not "*mei'eit Hashem*," "from the Lord." God does not usually answer our prayers by sending us miraculous deliverance or depositing a fortune at our doorstep. Instead, the experience of being with God, of entrusting our confidence in Him, of being aware of his presence at all times, gives us the strength to reorient our lives, to redirect all our energies, to refocus all our desires towards Him. This was the way in which Jacob's prayer was answered and his *eizer* came to him from the God who was the Creator of heaven and earth. Even as he prayed to God, saying, "As You helped my parents, so help me O God," and his prayer was answered when God proved to be his *eizer*, by bringing out the best in him – so may our prayers be answered.

We too pray for the divine *eizer*. Our hope is that He will grant us that same assistance whereby, as a result, we shall be the beneficiaries of the enlightenment of our eyes and the stability of our feet.

Behar

God or Mercury?[1]

The major portion of this morning's *sidra* deals with mundane, prosaic financial law – the disposition of real estate, the law of *Shemita* (the sabbatical law which controls agricultural development), loans and debtors and creditors, and the care and treatment of the poor and the indigent.

And then – at the very conclusion – we find an abrupt shift from a Torah for businessmen to the great and timeless religious principle which is so often repeated in the Torah and is one of its sacred fundamentals: "Ye shall make you no idols, neither shall ye rear you up a graven image, or a pillar" (Leviticus 26:1). And here the student of Torah wonders: What does real estate and commerce have to do with idolatry? What is the relation of illegitimate business dealings to icons?

Our Rabbis (*Sifra, Behar* 6:9) were in all probability as vexed by this passage as we are. And that is why they clearly identified the idol here intended by the Torah. They maintained that in this verse the Torah was referring to *Markulis*, a pagan god also known as "Mercury" or "Hermes."

---

1. May 17, 1958.

And with this interpretation of the Sages, the Biblical passage assumes new dimensions and becomes extremely meaningful to Jews of all times, and for us as well. For Mercury, *Markulis*, was the pagan god of the merchants, the idol of commerce. And what the Torah thus tells us is that if Torah is to be just ceremony, just synagogue procedure, just dignified ritual, and not a way of life which governs our conduct in business and trade as well as in shul – then we are no better than the worshippers of *Markulis*. For if God and Torah have no place in the professional life and business life of the Jew, then such a Jew is in effect worshipping business and trade as an end in itself, a devout communicant in the cult of Mercury, god of commerce.

This is the challenge of today's *sidra*: either God or Mercury. There is no middle position. Either you are a Jew all day and all week, or you are a pagan even when covered by a big *tallis*. Either one welcomes the judgment and teaching of Torah in one's conduct in trade and relations with business associates and charity contributions and everyday life – or it is as if one had worshipped the very idols so repugnant to our whole religion. When you look up to God in the shul and disregard Him in the marketplace, you have effectively killed the whole spirit of Judaism.

Of course, this does not mean that there are those who insist that religion should be confined to the Temples and that one should be consciously dishonest in his personal dealings – of course not. Everyone is against dishonesty and for good citizenship. But that is perhaps why the peculiar form of religious service of the idol Mercury was stoning him. You served Mercury by throwing rocks at him – in other words, when you denounce dishonesty, when you reject open lack of ethics, but at the same time immunize business life from the word of Torah – you are still worshipping the idol! Yes, even when throwing rocks at Mercury one worships him, provided that his domain – business and commerce – is kept out of God's jurisdiction.

And this worship of Mercury is an unfortunate development of modern times in Jewish life. Before the Emancipation, Jewish life was able to boast a healthy wholesomeness. All aspects of life, without exception, were treated from the point of view of Torah. In other words, the Jew looked on all problems from the point of view of God. Torah controlled the diet, guided sexual expression, determined financial questions, regulated prices, adjudicated disputes, approved or disapproved of contracts.

But in modern times, Judaism became fragmentized. Judaism became a matter of where you prayed, not how you lived; what *siddur* you used, not how regularly you paid employees or bills; how long was your *Shemone Esrei*, not how faithfully you worked for your salary; how good a tenor you got as a cantor, not how sincere your *davening* was; how ferociously you destroyed a competitor or "took in" a customer, not how much of your profits you gave to charity. Our whole *sidra* of this morning was forgotten, and business life became Godless – or better, became itself an object of worship and blind obedience.

And so Jews rejected the Lord, God of Israel, and accepted Mercury, god of commerce.

Why did this split between religion and life come about, this shrinkage of the area of Torah's influence? Probably it was part of the secularization of life in general. But more probably it was a Christian influence, an influence which gave religion a monopoly on relations to God, and relegated to Caesar a virtual monopoly on things relating to Caesar. But whatever the source of this split, it spells a tragedy for Jews – for they became worshippers of Mercury, the god of commerce.

What is necessary for the revitalization of Jewry in our day is a new appreciation of the fact that Judaism, unlike Christianity, is not relegated to one holy place and one holy day. When a local Jewish fraternal and social organization organizes a baseball picnic on Shabbat, it is violating the integrity, the wholeness of Jewish life. When another group, part of a great nation-wide organization, organizes a golf tournament on a Jewish fast-day and serves a luscious *treif* dinner – it reveals its paganism, especially when it resents a rabbi rearing his head out of the pulpit and extending it into the secular clubs and their activities. And even golf itself must be treated as part of a way of life – that is, it too is not immune from Jewish opinion. That is why a country club must conduct itself Jewishly, both in matters of diet and holidays and business-wise.

Every morning we say: "A man must always be (*le'olam yeheh*) God-fearing, in private and in public." Generally we take that as meaning that not only must a man be God-fearing in public, where all can see him, but even in private, where no one else can check on him. I beg to change that emphasis – not only in private, not only in the intimate matters of the heart, not only in the strict secrecy that guards a man's prayer and in the innermost communication of his heart with his Creator must a man be religious – but also in public, in the market place, in the professional office, in the store, in the club, in the factory, before the bar.

There is no dearth of Jewish law on social and business relationships. Under the influence of this split, of this shrinkage, of the effect of this Mercury cult, some of us may be surprised at how great a literature we have concerning activity outside the synagogue. All one has to do is open a *Shulḥan Arukh* or a Rambam. There are laws of prayer and interest; *tefillin* and profiteering; *tallis* and sexual relations; *mezuza* and tax evasion; Shabbat and larceny. Rabbi Yehuda Leib Maimon has recently calculated that there exist today over 100,000 *teshuvot* (responses to questions, or case histories) relating to social law or business law alone!

We today must return to this fuller and greater understanding of Torah, as it is presented to us in today's *sidra*. By subjecting all of life to God's influence, we will have smashed the statues of Mercury, instead of merely throwing pebbles at it. By opening all areas of our existence to the teachings of our tradition, we will have acted as genuine Jews, not as half and one-quarter Jews. We will have grown to the fuller spiritual stature of one who realizes that "the earth is the Lord's, and the fullness thereof" (Psalms 24:1), and therefore all life must be lived so as not to be embarrassed by His presence. "A man must always be God-fearing, in private and in public" – not only in private but also in public. Then and only then can we conclude with the phrase, *"umodeh al ha'emet,"* "acknowledging the truth" – then will we have understood the great truths, the *emet*, of Judaism; *"vedover emet bilvavo,"* "and speak truth in his heart" – and then will the truths of Torah be not superficial and external, but then they will have penetrated to the very innermost depths of the heart, so that *"veyashkeim veyomar,"* so that we may rise each morning and say, with full knowledge and commitment, *"ribon kol ha'amim"* – you, O God, are the Master of the whole world, and nothing is beyond Your greatness and Your scrutiny.

Our War on Poverty[1]

O ne of the key verses in this morning's *sidra* reads, "If your brother becomes poor, and sells (*umakhar*) some of his possessions (*mei'aḥuzato*), then shall his nearest relative come and redeem that which his brother has sold (*vega'al et mimkar aḥiv*)" (Leviticus 25:25).

This verse may be read on three levels. First, there is the obvious, literal meaning of the verse which is halakhic, or legal. If a man is reduced to such poverty that he feels he must sell his ancestral land, then his nearest relative must repurchase it for him, so that the land will remain within the tribe and family, and not be left to strangers.

A second level is the moral one. It speaks in general of responsibility to one's family. It reminds us that no matter how ambivalent the feelings of relatives are to each other, nevertheless, in the long run, one's closest relatives are one's best friends. Parents and children, brothers and sisters, may harbor their private resentments, but in the final analysis and in times of crisis it is one's relatives to whom one turns, and rightly so.

---

1. May 22, 1965.

Finally, the same verse can be read on a more fundamental, spiritual level. It has wider Jewish implications and it is these upon which I propose to elaborate this morning. This spiritual interpretation was given by one of the giants of the early Hasidic movement, Rabbi Elimelech of Lizensk, the author of *No'am Elimelekh*. He derives this novel insight by playing on two words in our verse. The Hebrew word *"makhar"* he interprets not literally as, "And he shall sell," but in the sense of *"hitmakheir,"* "And he shall become estranged." And the word *"ahuz"* refers, he says, not to one's ancestral land or real estate, but rather to one's ancestral spiritual heritage. Thus, the verse reads as follows: If you brother becomes reduced to such extreme spiritual poverty that he is estranged from the heritage of his fathers, he feels distant and cut off from the sacred traditions of Israel, then we, his fellow Jews, who are his closest relatives, must become his redeemer; we must redeem the "heritage" for our brothers who are "estranged" and hence find themselves religiously impoverished. This is our "war on poverty."

The principle Rabbi Elimelech of Lizensk finds in this verse seems true enough – in fact it would even appear to be a truism. Apparently it is but a restatement of the ancient Jewish principles of *"kol Yisrael areivim zeh bazeh"* (*Shevu'ot* 39a), that all Israelites are responsible one for the other. It is a well known theme in Judaism, and one that accounts for the cohesion of the House of Israel.

Yet, today that principle is not at all self-evident. It must be enunciated and articulated in many forms and fashions, for we have failed to abide by it. This failure has come about for two reasons.

First, we Jews of the Western world suffer from a fundamental misunderstanding. We have misinterpreted a doctrine that is a cornerstone of Western civilization and American democracy. That doctrine is: "Religion is a matter of the individual conscience."

Indeed, that statement constitutes an immortal contribution to the history of mankind. We Jews, who have through the ages been the perennial victims of religious bigotry and oppression, have become the greatest beneficiaries of this doctrine. Both Jews and Judaism gladly assent to that proposition. The *Halakha* approves it – it rules out any coercion on matters of *dei'ot*, of conscience or belief. All Jews can agree with this theme as it was recently restated, in homey fashion, by the president of a Midwestern university: "Religion is like a toothbrush – every man should have one and use it regularly, but should not try to force it on anybody else!"

However, we have made an error in carrying this idea beyond its proper borders. We have erred in assuming that because we ought not to use coercion, therefore we ought not to have concern with the religious life of our neighbors; because we ought not to force anyone to faith therefore we ought not to care about the spiritual environment in which we live. Some people carry this to an extreme which, to any sensible and mature human being, seems ludicrous – they declare, in a mood of pious liberalism, "I shall let my child choose his own religion." As if the child, by virtue of blissful ignorance, can manufacture a viable religion which has taken the rest of civilization several millennia to formulate!

The reaction against religious oppression, therefore, often drives us to the opposite extreme, to a complete disclaimer of responsibility for the spiritual condition of our fellow men. And so we declare, "I am not God's messenger, not His *shaliaḥ.*" Yet that is one of the most un-Jewish statements possible. For every human being, by virtue of his being created in "the image of God," is automatically a messenger of God. And every Jew, by virtue of being a member of a people that met God on Mount Sinai, is automatically an ambassador of Judaism both to fellow Jews and to all of mankind.

A second reason for this abdication of the function of religious responsibility is due to the nature of Orthodox Judaism in our own times. For we Orthodox Jews have turned too insular, too isolationist. Because of the attrition of the last two centuries, and because of the various forms of "Judaism" that are indeed destructive of Torah, we have turned defensive. We have largely withdrawn into ourselves because of the fact that so many alien and baneful values, crassly materialistic and dangerously immoral, impinge and intrude upon our lives and homes and schools by ever more effective means of mass communication. Television and advertising, in general, force upon the attention of our children and ourselves ideals of behavior and modes of conduct which are repugnant to all we stand for and have cherished through the ages. Our reaction has been to fight such influences by withdrawing. As a result, all too often we have given the impression, both in Israel and in America, of oscillating between unconcern for other Jews and coercion of those who are not of our persuasion. We seem to vacillate between isolation and reaction.

Both these impressions are false – and to the very limited extent that they may be true, we must totally disabuse ourselves of them. But the image persists, and we have done precious little to disprove the contentions of our opponents. We must therefore undertake to create, by example, a new image. We must learn to be aggressive without being offensive; we must be not ingrown, but outgoing. We must redirect our energies from licking our wounds and fighting back to reaching the masses of uncommitted Jews, many of whom do not even know what an Orthodox Jew is.

"Vega'al et mimkar aḥiv" – we must redeem the heritage of Judaism for our brothers who have sold it all too cheaply. This is the task and the obligation that God and destiny place upon us who consider ourselves Orthodox. Our duty is to redeem – for those who will not redeem are themselves condemned to remain unredeemed!

How shall we redeem this Jewish heritage for our poor, estranged brethren?

First, by education. It may be revealing to some people to learn that our far-flung and wide-spread network of day schools does not cater exclusively to children of Orthodox parents. Large numbers of them come from homes which are totally ignorant of Judaism. By supporting our day schools – almost any one of them! – we are in a sense reaching out in a most positive and constructive way into the hearts and homes of uncommitted Jews. We do so again by providing for the education of those who are not in day schools but beyond the age of *Bar Mitzva*, as we in the Center do in sponsoring the Manhattan Hebrew High School. We do it through such organizations as Yavneh, which reaches out to young people on the campuses of this country. We ought to do so through other means, making use of the latest communications technology in order to reach ever-wider masses of Jews who are completely ignorant of all that the tradition of Judaism stands for.

Second, we must express our spiritual co-responsibility for our fellow Jews by concern for the welfare of all Jews, and not only their spiritual well-being. Orthodoxy must never become a specialist of the spirit exclusively. If we wish to exert an influence in religion, we must identify ourselves with the totality of our people. It was the great founder of the *Mussar* movement Rabbi Israel Salanter who said that every man's first concern should be his own spiritual health and the material welfare of his neighbor. His second concern ought to be his own material health and his neighbor's spiritual state. Only by taking a very genuine and authentic concern in every Jew, and in the collectivity of all Jews, by cherishing the totality of Israel, we will be able to bring about the desired spiritual renaissance.

Third, the way to exercise such an influence is by example. The Orthodox Jew must lead an exemplary moral and ethical life. The more we are identified with traditional Judaism, the greater our reputation as Orthodox Jews, the greater the obligation upon us. Even a superficial perusal of the first parts of Maimonides' Code of Jewish Law, the *Mishneh Torah*, will confide to us that the more one is identified as a religious Jew, the greater his responsibilities. When any other kind of Jew transgresses a law, it is merely accounted a transgression of that particular law. When an Orthodox Jew, however, especially one who is somewhat learned, violates the same law, he is at the same time guilty of a far greater sin known as *hillul Hashem*, the desecration of God's Name. For, in itself, his lack of ethics reflects upon the entirety of the Jewish tradition, upon God's very Name! Conversely, when we observe the highest ethical ideals, we have performed *kiddush Hashem*, the sanctification of God's Name.

All this holds true not only for chosen leaders of Orthodoxy or for impersonal organizations or schools, but for every single individual in this synagogue and in every other. Every Jew, no matter what level of observance, must establish contacts with other Jews and attempt to exercise the benign influence of one's own faith upon all others. Let none of us fall back upon the excuse that we are not sufficiently observant ourselves. Just as when it comes to philanthropy people cannot excuse themselves from the obligation to share what they have with others on the grounds that they are not the wealthiest people in the community, so one need not be a perfect saint in order to respond to the challenge of exercising a spiritual influence upon others. We must, indeed, "talk religion" with other fellow Jews – provided, of course, that we inform ourselves first of all that we should know.

This, then, is the act of redemption which our *sidra* calls upon us to perform. If we do it, and if we do it properly, then we will have fulfilled not only the normal interpretation but also the special Hasidic insight into the principle which we mentioned earlier: "*kol Yisrael areivim zeh bazeh.*" Normally this means, "All Israelites are responsible one for the other." The Hasidic addition is to read the word "*areivim*" as meaning not only "responsible," but also "sweet." If we will show our spiritual responsibility for our fellow Jews, then indeed we shall be sweet to our fellow Jews – "All Israelites must be sweet one to another."

Having done that, having discharged our responsibility and shown ourselves sweet and gracious to every fellow Jew, we will have redeemed the estranged heritage for our brethren.

And then, in return, Almighty God will redeem us – "*uva leTzion go'el.*" May indeed the Redeemer come to Zion (Isaiah 59:20). Amen.

Sons and Servants[1]

After banning a permanent slave class among Israelites by legislating that every Israelite servant must be emancipated on the Jubilee year, the Torah offers its reason: "For the children of Israel are servants (*avadim*) unto Me, they are My servants" (Leviticus 25:55).

The title "*eved*" or "servant" is obviously meant in an honorific sense. Thus, the highest encomium that the Bible offers for Moses, that most superior of all prophets and human is, "*Moshe eved Hashem*," "Moses the servant of the Lord" (Deuteronomy 34:5).

There is also another description of man's relationship to God used by the Torah: "You are *banim*, sons (or children) to the Lord your God" (Deuteronomy 14:1). So we have an interesting biblical typology: *ben* and *eved*, son and servant, two symbols or archetypes of the religious personality.

Unquestionably, in one sense *eved* (servant) is superior to *ben* (son). "Servant" indicates one who has no natural relationship, but has come to his master-father from without. The *eved* of the Lord

---

1. May 19, 1973.

is one who therefore comes to the *Adon Olam* (the Eternal Master) voluntarily, utterly of his own free will, ready to subjugate himself to the will of the Almighty, to suppress his ego and restrain his desires in manifest and meaningful commitment to God. "Son," however, is one who, as it were, was born into this relationship with his Father. From this point of view, the proselyte is superior to the native born Jew! Indeed, in a famous responsum by Maimonides to Obadiah the Proselyte who complained that his Jewish teacher was rebuking him and insulting him by reminding him of his pagan origin, Maimonides says that the teacher should be ashamed of himself and should stand in awe of the student who is a proselyte and who came to the Almighty of his own free will rather than being born into it naturally.

And yet the weight of the Jewish tradition offers the reverse judgment and maintains that the category of *ben* is superior to the category of *eved*. Thus, Rabbi Akiva teaches in *Avot* 3:14, "Beloved is Israel that they were called sons of the Almighty."

What is the difference between these two conceptions, that of man as *eved* and as *ben* to God? Let us discuss three of them.

The first analysis is objective rather than subjective. It tells us how Judaism considers man as such, in all his weakness and his frailty, rather than how man conceives of himself subjectively as a religious being in his relationship to God.

And here we turn to Rabbi Akiva himself in a fascinating dialogue, recorded in the Talmud (*Bava Batra* 10a), between Rabbi Akiva and his Roman tormentor, who was later to become the executioner of the venerable sage:

> This question was posed by Tyranus Rufus the wicked to Rabbi Akiva: If indeed your God loves the poor, as you say, why does He not provide for them? Rabbi Akiva answered: So that we might thereby be saved from punishment of Gehinom (for in sharing one's substance with the poor and in helping the disadvantaged we affirm our worth in life and thus save ourselves from eternal perdition). To this Tyranus Rufus replied: On the contrary, for doing so you deserve to go to Gehinom! I will offer you a parable: It can be compared to a human king who became angry

with one of his servants and placed him in prison and ordered that he be given no food and no drink. Along came another man and brought in food and drink to the imprisoned slave. When the king hears about this, is he not angry with this stranger who violated his rules? And you Israelites are called servants, as it is written, "For the children or Israel are servants unto Me." To this Rabbi Akiva responded: On the contrary, I will offer you a different parable. It can be compared to a human king who became angry with his son and placed him in prison and commanded that he not be given any food and drink. When the king hears about this, is he not so happy that he is willing to send a gift to this stranger? And we are called sons, as it is written, "You are sons to the Lord your God."

If we see man as an *eved*, as a passive and servile creation of God, then we are fatalists. Then we must declare that whatever exists is the inexorable will of God, and that is the way it must remain. In that case, the poor must remain poor, the sick must remain miserable, and the sufferers must continue to suffer, all because this is the will of God. Any attempt to relieve or improve their condition is considered sacrilegious and a blasphemous interference with God's plans for the world. This philosophy of man as *eved* is the most convenient ideology for the establishment, the "haves" to keep control over the "have-nots."

But Jews do not subscribe to this *eved* anthropology; that is the way Tyranus Rufus and his Romans and pagans speak. Rabbi Akiva, however, declared that man is a *ben*, that people are children of God, and then we must interpret all evil and suffering as a challenge to us to remove it, as if God did indeed create a flawed world, but willed that His human creatures look upon each other as children of God and therefore free the imprisoned and the disadvantaged and the hungry and the poor from their distress and affliction. God made this world, but He is anxious that we make it better. God started this world, but he wants us to complete it.

So whereas man should see himself as an *eved*, he must always see others as *ben*. Therefore, in general, as Rabbi Akiva taught, *ben* is superior to *eved*, and this theory becomes the foundation of all of

Judaism which urges us to treat every person as a child of God – as a brother and sister – as one whose welfare and happiness God desires and commands us to enhance.

There is a second definition of this dichotomy of *eved-ben*. In this definition, the two terms describe not only how we ought to view other men, but they are archetypes of how a Jew should relate to God and to Judaism. Thus, as one great Jew of recent generations, Rabbi Barukh haLevi Epstein, said, the *eved* does only what he has to, only what he must, only what he is told to do; whereas the *ben* seeks to satisfy his father even beyond what he was ordered to do. The *eved* does what the master demands; the son does what the father wants. The *eved* is interested in the commandment alone; the *ben* also seeks to perform the will of his creator. As an example: The Torah commands that whenever we have a four-cornered garment that we affix thereto the *tzitzit* (fringes). The *eved* will say: Since I do not have such a garment, it is unnecessary for me to wear the *tzitzit*. And he is right, halakhically. But he is a minimalist, doing only what he must and no more. The *ben*, under similar circumstances, will seek out a four-cornered garment in order to be able to perform the law of affixing the *tzitzit*. The son is a maximalist, he goes beyond what he must – he reaches out for the supererogatory.

The third analysis is based upon a modification of what the Zohar teaches. The Zohar (*Ra'aya Mehemna,* Leviticus, *Behar* 111:2) tells us that both terms are indicative of high religious personalities that appear to be different, but ultimately the mystery of each is really one. The *eved* is a description of conduct or behavior, one who performs all the commandments fully, whereas the *ben* not only performs the commandments, but feels at home with God. The *ben* is "*mehapes beginzei aviv,*" he knows all the nooks and corners of his father's will in practice, but also wants to know as much as he can about his father. What the Zohar means is that the *eved* is one who performs the *Halakha,* who does all the practical commandments, whereas the *ben* is the one who pursues the *sitrei Torah,* the mysteries of the Torah, or, in other words, is an initiate into the Kabbala.

In contemporary terms, we may modify that statement to refer to not one who is a mystic, but rather it means that the *eved* is one who practices alone, but not necessarily with feeling; whereas the *ben* is one who invests emotion and feeling and love. The *eved* is a Jew who observes and gives and participates, but you can feel the icicles hanging from his heart. The *ben* is a Jew who not only observes and gives and participates, but also worries and loves and feels, who puts heart and soul into what he does.

We thus have three interpretations of the distinctions between the terms *ben* and *eved*. To summarize: The first definition is that, relating to others, we must seem to them as sons, and therefore as individuals whom God loves and whom God wants us to help out of their distress even if they deserve their misery – and not as servants whom God does not care about, or desires that they remain in their punishment. The second is that the *eved* is a minimalist who does only what he must, whereas the *ben* is a person who goes beyond his minimal requirements. And finally, the *eved* is a Jew who carries out everything in practice, but not necessarily with the feeling and inner participation that characterize the son.

As a rabbi of an Orthodox congregation, it is often my very unpleasant duty to reproach not only my congregation but the entire Orthodox community, and especially what we call Modern Orthodox Jews. Today, however, for the sake of proper proportion and perspective and to complete the picture, permit me to assert that despite all its shortcomings it is this community of Orthodox and especially Modern Orthodox Jews which, in the context of our times, represents the quality of *ben* as opposed to *eved*.

At a time such as ours when other Jews who were long blind to the Jewish destiny have become hysterical and speak so breathlessly of "Jewish identity" and "Jewish survival," Orthodox Jews go far beyond that, and are striving for infinitely more than these bare minimum qualities of identity and survival. "You are sons to the Lord your God," and our concern as children of Israel and of God is with the study of Torah and the performance of *mitzvot*, not merely with that elusive and intangible and insubstantial "identity" and "survival."

Moreover, by the same token, while other fine Jews are panic-stricken and motivated by a fear for the Jewish future, grasping at all kinds of artificial devices, and acting as if merely crash-financing a program which reaches out "to the young" will solve all problems,

Orthodox Jews approach their Judaism not exclusively as a communal matter, but also with *ahava*, with inner feeling and total commitment as a supreme personal way of life which demands warmth and love.

And at least for Modern Orthodox Jews, for most of them and for most of the time, although not for all of them all the time, we have learned how to view other, recalcitrant Jews as *banim* and not as *avadim*. We may be distressed at their non-observance and their lack of religion, but we recognize them as children of God, and therefore as our brothers and our sisters. And we shall not give up on them!

Within the community that embodies these conceptions and that typifies these attitudes, the most representative segment is Yeshiva University, an institution which is more than seventy-five years old. Orthodoxy in America, and especially Orthodoxy that has come to terms with the modern experience, is unthinkable without Yeshiva University.

An amazing thing happened several months ago, and the Israeli press commented in almost disbelief upon this event. When Prime Minister Golda Meir visited this country, she received an honorary degree from Yeshiva University. After her reception, in the office of Dr. Belkin, Golda Meir wept! She said that she had never seen such a youth, that she had never believed it could exist even in Israel. She saw thousands of young men and women, an overwhelmingly impressive community, which left her breathless. Here were young people devoted to maximal Jewishness, not to just surviving or identifying; young people who obviously were effusive in their love and devotion for Israel and Torah and the State of Israel, with warmth and enthusiasm. And here were Orthodox Jews, fully committed to Torah and Judaism, who nevertheless had about them an openness to other Jews – not by avoiding the issues, not by being pliant and submissive, not by accepting uncritically anything that all Israelis or the government or Golda Meir does or says, but young people who are aware that all Jews are sons to the Lord our God.

Why did Golda weep? Because she discovered then and there, in the encounter with Yeshiva University, that "beloved is Israel that they were called sons of the Almighty" – that these charming and lovely young people were indeed children of God and of Israel. She saw these vibrant and enthusiastic, uncompromised and proud Jews, Jews whose way of life she once may have thought existed as cultural relics only in Mea Shearim or else in the Russian ghettos she left as a child – who nevertheless had not abandoned the Jewish tradition, who were able to combine it with a worldly outlook, who were college and graduate university students. And withal, they are *benei* and *benot Torah*.

She saw before her not *avadim* but *banim*. Indeed, that was something to cry about, to shed tears of joy about – for she had found sons, not merely servants.

In Praise of Impracticality[1]

Our *sidra* opens with the words, "And the Lord spoke to Moses at Mount Sinai (*behar Sinai*), saying..." (Leviticus 25:1). What follows this introduction is a portion that deals with the laws of *shemita*, the sabbatical year, when the land must lie fallow and all debts be remitted.

The Rabbis were intrigued by one word in that opening verse: the word *"behar,"* "on the mountain." Why this special reference to Mount Sinai at this time? The question as they phrased it has come over into Yiddish and Hebrew as an idiomatic way of saying, "What does one thing have to do with the other?" Thus (*Torat Kohanim*, as quoted by Rashi): *"ma inyan shemita eitzel Har Sinai?"* "What connection is there between the sabbatical laws and Mount Sinai?" Were not all the laws and commandments enunciated at Mount Sinai? Why then this special mention of *shemita* in association with Mount Sinai?

Rashi quotes the answer provided by the Rabbis. Permit me, however, to offer an alternative answer: Although Judaism is action-geared,

---

1. May 6, 1972.

oriented to the improvement of humanity and society; although it has a high moral quotient; although it addresses itself to the very real problems of imperfect beings and suffering society; although, in contrast to certain other religions, it is more this-worldly – nevertheless, this concern with the real and the immediate and the empirical has a limit. Not everything in Judaism has to be as practical as an American businessman's profit-and-loss sheet or as "relevant" as the social activists and the radicals would like it to be. Judaism may not be ancient history – but neither is it journalism.

And this we see from the piquant fact that the laws of *shemita* were given specifically at Mount Sinai. Laws known as *mitzvot hateluyot ba'aretz*, commandments whose fulfillment is dependent upon the Land of Israel, were given to the people of Israel before they ever arrived in *Eretz Yisrael*, the Land of Israel! Agricultural laws were now given, in all their details, to a nomadic tribe without farms, without roots in the soil. Consider what the laws of *shemita* sounded like to our grandparents as they surrounded Mount Sinai, that bare desert mountain. They must have appeared weird, irrelevant, out of place, impertinent.

And yet, what was true of *shemita* at Mount Sinai is true of all the commandments at all times. They may seem hopelessly impractical, untimely, and irrelevant to the cold-eyed and hard-headed person, and yet they are the Law of the Lord, obligatory upon Jews at all times and all places.

Indeed, there is hardly anything as irrelevant as the piddling relevancy of the coldly practical person. Show me the man who sees only what is before his eyes, and I will show you a man who cannot see beyond his nose!

What does this praise of the impractical teach us?

First, it tells us simply that there are things that are of value in and of themselves, not only because they are instrumental or lead to other things. Thus, some of the commandments may restrain one's destructiveness. Others may lead one to improve society or one's own soul or help the disadvantaged. But some are valuable simply because they were commanded by God. No other reason is necessary.

The same is true of knowledge. There are some kinds of knowledge which may lead to invention and enhance the health of an individual and his convenience. But science is more than technology. There is also such a thing as knowledge for its own sake, knowledge acquired in order to satisfy the natural intellectual curiosity of mankind.

A week ago, Apollo 16 returned from its trip to the moon. Except for those Americans who are so benumbed by the sensational that after the first time a thing is done it becomes a dreadful bore, the exploits of the astronauts kept the world enraptured. And yet consider what a monumental irrelevance the whole project is! The government spends millions of dollars, some of the brightest men in the world donate their talents, three men risk their lives – all in order to study the structure of remote rocks so that we might formulate a theory of when the moon was created and how old it is. "So what?" one might ask. And the answer is: "So everything!"

Yes, there may be legitimate questions about the priorities in our national budget. That is not now our concern. But without a doubt, knowledge, for its own sake, must not be deprecated. The real point, to a small-minded person, sometimes appears to be beside the point.

And the same is true in Judaism. There is the study of Torah for the sake of performance of the *mitzvot,* or the sake of cohesion of the community, or the sake of raising the level of Jewish observance. But the highest concept of Torah study remains *Torah lishma,* Torah for its own sake. Here too, there may be a question of priorities in determining the subject matter of Torah. But there is no denying the ultimate and high value of *Torah lishma,* of study for its own sake.

It was the Jerusalem Talmud (*Ḥagiga* 2:1) that attributed to the most notorious heretic in Jewish history the opposition to "otherworldly study of Torah." Elisha ben Abuya, known as Aḥer ("the other one"), is said to have stormed into a classroom, rudely interrupted the teacher, and shouted at the students: "What are you doing here? Why are you wasting your time in such irrelevant material as Torah? You, you must be a builder; you must be a carpenter; you ought to become a fisherman, and you should be a tailor. Do something useful in your lives!" The great heretic was an eminently practical man…

Of course, I do not mean to be cute by espousing impracticality and advocating irrelevance. Total irrelevance is deadening to the spirit and results in what philosophers call solipsism, the divorce from the outside world and experience and the introversion into oneself – and impracticality can become nothing but a semantic excuse for inefficiency and incompetence. What I do mean is that relevance is a good, but not the only one or even the most important one. And while practicality is necessary for the execution of ideals, dreams and visions need not be pre-restrained in the Procrustean bed of a mercantile mentality.

The second point is that sometimes the apparently remote does contain highly significant and very real dimensions, but it is our narrow vision and restricted understanding that does not allow us to expose these obscure insights. *Kashrut* sometimes is ridiculed in this modern age because it appears superfluous when we consider the sanitary facilities we possess. And yet, those who understand *kashrut* realize that it has so little to do with sanitation and has so very much to say about reverence for life – and this, in a world in which life is losing its value, in which the approval of abortions is moving into the encouragement of euthanasia. *Shatnez* and *kilayim*, the prohibitions against mixing various garments or seeds or animals, has always been held up as a paradigm of non-rational commandments, and yet today we realize how much they have to say to us about ecology and the preservation of the separate species of the universe. The Sabbath laws are meant not only to give us a day of rest, because Sunday in modern America can accomplish that as well. It does tell us that we are not the by-products of a cosmic accident, that we owe our existence to God, and must therefore curb our insufferable pride and collective arrogance.

So, these and many other such illustrations remind us of the need to search beneath the surface of Judaism for teachings that are eminently pertinent.

Third, we must be future-oriented. We must have faith that what is genuinely irrelevant now may someday become most relevant and meaningful as a result of our ability to carry on heroically despite present irrelevance and impracticality. What today seems visionary may prove indispensable to tomorrow's very real need.

The Rabbis were fond of saying, "The words of Torah and the Sages are 'poor' in one place (*bimkom zeh*) and 'rich' in another (*bimkom aḥer*)" (*Yerushalmi Rosh HaShana* 3:5). By this they meant to say that sometimes the text of Torah will seem utterly narrow and superficial, teaching very little indeed. It is only when we compare it with another text, in another context, that we can appreciate how genuinely deep and insightful it really is. I would like to paraphrase that passage, switching from "*makom*" to "*zeman*" – thus: It sometimes happens that the words of Torah in one epoch may seem to be thin and insignificant; it is only later, at another time, that the same words stand revealed as possessing unspeakable richness of insight and teaching.

Take the most striking example: the hope for Jerusalem, whose fifth anniversary of liberation we celebrate later this week.

If we have the privilege to commemorate the reunion of people and city, of Israel and Jerusalem, we must acknowledge our debt to a hundred generations of Jews and Jewesses who since the year 70 have been wild dreamers, impractical idealists, possessed of visions impossible of execution; Jews who turned to Jerusalem three times a day in prayer; who when they ate bread thanked God for bread and for Jerusalem; who mentioned Jerusalem when they fasted and when they feasted; who brought little packets of dust of Jerusalem during their lifetime in order to take it along with them in their coffins on their long journey to eternity; who arose at midnight for *tikun ḥatzot*, to lament over Jerusalem, and at every happy occasion promised to return there.

If we live in Jerusalem today, it is because of those unsophisticated visionaries who wanted at least to die in it.

If we can visit Jerusalem this year, it is thanks to those otherworldly dreamers who sang "*leshana haba'a biYerushalayim*" – at least let us be there next year.

If we can happily laugh – "*az yimalei seḥok pinu,*" "then our mouth will be full of laughter" (Psalms 126:2) – it is in large measure the work of those who did not realize how irrelevant they were, how impossible their dreams were, and who prayed to return there, thus daring and braving and risking the derisive laughter of legions of practical people who simply "knew" that we were finished, and that Jerusalem would never become a Jewish city again.

It is only because of generations of bridegrooms who concluded every wedding by stomping on a glass, its shattering fragments recalling the *ḥurban habayit* (the destruction of Jerusalem), and proclaiming, "If I forget you O Jerusalem, let my right hand fail" (Psalms 137:5), that today we can defy the whole world, East and West, and say: Never again shall you separate us from Jerusalem, not Capitalists and not Communists, not Muslims and not even Christians who have lately discovered that Jerusalem is important to them.

Jerusalem Day is a tribute to this special Jewish brand of impracticality and irrelevance.

So, *"ma inyan shemita eitzel Har Sinai?"* – What is the association or connection between the sabbatical laws and Mount Sinai? First, it is to tell us that not everything need be relevant; second, that not everything that appears irrelevant really is; and third, that what is irrelevant today may be the most important fact of life tomorrow.

This lesson too is part of the heritage of Sinai. Indeed, without it all the rest is in jeopardy. With it, all the rest will prevail too, *bimheira beyameinu*, speedily in our day.

Beḥukotai

Having the Capacity to Listen[1]

T he *tokhaha*, that terrible portion of today's *sidra* which predicts the horrible consequences attendant upon the rejection of God by Israel, and which has unfortunately been proven true to the last detail in our own lifetime, is divided into two parts. Both begin with similar expressions: "*ve'im lo tishme'u li*," "And if you will not listen to Me" (Leviticus 26:14) and "*ve'im bizot lo tishme'u li*," "And if in all this you will not listen to Me" (Leviticus 26:27). Both, therefore, are introduced with the pre-condition that these will happen "*im lo tishme'u li*," if you will not obey God.

But our Rabbis saw in these words more than a plain warning against disobedience. That is why they commented (*Sifra, Behukotai* 2:1), "'*lo tishme'u – lemidrash hakhamim*," that this disobedience refers particularly to rejection and neglect of the interpretations of the Sages. For the lack of practice is a result of the lack of study. Or, more generally and more clearly, the lack of obedience is a result of the lack of proper listening. The word "*shamo'a*," in Hebrew, is a homonym – it means

1. May 14, 1955.

both "obey" and "listen." The core of the trouble, the primary cause of disobedience, is faulty listening. That is what makes for a *tohakha*.

Hasidim relate that a Hasid once came to his rebbe and asked the following question: The *Mishna* (*Avot* 6:2) states that, "Every day a heavenly voice emanates from Mount Horeb, proclaiming 'Woe to the people because of the affront to the Torah.'" The Hasid therefore asked his rebbe, "If the reason for this daily divine voice is to inspire *teshuva*, to encourage repentance, then everyone should hear it. If no one can hear it, what is the use of this daily divine announcement?" The rebbe answered with a parable: "A father who was a merchant once took his son on a sales trip. They passed through a thick forest, and the boy spied beautiful black and red berries and very much wanted to pick them. However, the father told his son that there was no time for them to stop, and they must continue riding on their wagon. The son, in response, replied that he will get off of the wagon, gather the berries, and the father should ride on slowly, and the son will catch up to him. The father responded that he feared his son would get lost. So the son suggested that every now and then he would call out and the father should answer, and when he's picked enough berries he would run to cover the lost ground. As the son left the wagon to go into the forest, the father told him: 'Remember son, if you hear the voice of your father and follow it, all will be well – you won't get lost. But if you do not listen to my voice, if you cannot hear the voice of your father, then you will get lost in this great forest.'"

We moderns have lost the capacity to listen. The divine voice calls out daily – we should be able to hear the voice of our Father – but the trouble is that we're not listening. This is dangerous and is symptomatic of desensitized souls, and God-forbid, it could forebode a terrible *tokhaha*.

The sociologist David Reisman, in his book *The Lonely Crowd*, speaks of our society as a wordy one, as one in which the flow of words from the mass-media of communication has become a veritable torrent. We're so busy talking, we do not listen. One may hear, physically, but that is purely automatic. Unless one listens, his hearing is of no value. Hearing a sermon or lecture is not the same as listening to it. Hearing the Torah reading is often automatic – listening to it is a creative act of the spirit. It involves deep study – it involves *midrash ḥakhamim*, a profound acquaintance with the interpretations of the Sages, a high sensitivity to their moral message.

A relative of mine is taking graduate work in education, and one of the courses he is taking is titled "Listening" – because the education of children involves more than talking to children and teaching them to talk. It involves listening to them – their voices, their laughter, their tempers, their weeping, and their very heartbeats – and teaching them to listen to the same in others. Real education requires listening with a spiritual stethoscope. It requires *midrash ḥakhamim*, true and profound wisdom.

The technique of most of psychiatry – certainly analysis – is largely a matter of listening – and that means more than just hearing. Listening to a troubled man or woman, as a rabbi too has frequent occasion to do, is – or can be – a highly creative and skillful act. That kind of listening is itself a *midrash ḥakhamim*, an act of wisdom.

In a similar way, just like in education and psychiatry, religion insists that every individual listen to one another – for the voice of the divine Father calls out every minute. It is up to us to listen, to rotate our antennae and set our receiving frequencies so that we can hear the divine message that is broadcast daily from Mount Horeb. That is why the Torah decreed that a man who willfully sells himself into permanent slavery must have his ear bored (Deuteronomy 15:17) – for that ear, the one that heard the voice of God saying that Israel is slave to God not to Man, did not hear and did not listen.

So what does it mean to listen? What can one hear when one is attuned, when one concentrates?

The person who has watched the ocean in the moonlight, who has been sensitive to the passing moods of the ocean – its tranquility alternating with unrequited passion and rage, its mysteriousness and its wisdom compounded with benevolence – that creature, if he listens, hears a voice. Through the great crash of the waves and white tumult of the foam, "the voice of the Lord is upon the waters" (Psalms 29:3).

An individual who has seen, personally or televised, the naked might, the brutal awe and raw splendor of an atomic bomb explosion, the release of all those overwhelming, primitive powers of nature – the gigantic might that lies dormant in every atom in this universe – he hears a voice too, a voice more permanent and more meaningful than the explosion of the bomb or the blare of the announcers' descriptions, a voice that cannot be measured in decibels: "The voice of the Lord is in might" (Psalms 29:4).

The human being who feels his heart flooded with warmth and joy and experiences aesthetic delight as he opens a sensitive soul to the message of hope that lies in every blade of grass, in every blossoming bud and growing leaf; the person whose heart swells with happiness as he sees the bare and prosaic streets of a wintery forest park turned into beauty-arched lanes bedecked with nature's finery and adorned with the poetry of growth – such an individual is listening. And as that individual listens, he hears: "The voice of the Lord is in beauty" (Psalms 29:4).

When an individual does all that, that person is not merely exercising the purely automatic geological function of hearing. Rather, that person is doing only what a human being can do: That individual is listening, is indulging in *midrash ḥakhamim*, in the exercise of wisdom.

When we bend our ears and listen to *kol Hashem*, to the voice of the Lord, in its various manifestations, we will not be lost in the forest of life.

"Hear O Israel" – nay, "Listen O Israel – the Lord our God is One" (Deuteronomy 6:4). Listen to His voice, and you will not be lost in the forest of *tokhaḥa*. Rather, "And thou shalt love the Lord thy God" (Deuteronomy 6:5) – that kind of listening leads to love, to a closer, warmer, happier bond between God and mankind.

The Tablets Within[1]

I t is well known that in Judaism we have two Torahs: the *Torah shebikhtav*, the Written Torah, that is, the Bible or Scripture; and the *Torah shebe'al peh*, the Oral Torah, the sacred tradition which ultimately was condensed in the literature of Talmud.

This morning I wish to commend your attention to a sub-division in the category of *Torah shebikhtav*, the Written Law. The difference between the Written and Oral Law is this: The Oral Law is expressed in terms of concept and ideas, whereas the Written Law is articulated in the form of letters. Now, Rabbi Shneur Zalman of Liadi, founder of the Habad movement in Hasidism, teaches (in his *Likutei Torah* to *Behukotai*) that the Written Torah comes in two kinds of letters. One he refers to simply as *ketiva*, writing or inscription. The second consists of *hakika*, engraving. When we write the words of the Torah on the Scroll of the Law, ink upon parchment – that is *ketiva*. *Hakika* refers not to writing with one substance upon another, but to engraving the letters upon the object itself, such as the two tablets Moses brought down

---

1. May 29, 1965.

from Mount Sinai bearing the Ten Commandments, or the twelve large stones upon which, towards the end of his days, he was commanded to engrave the words of the entire Torah and erect them on the shores of the Jordan River.

What is the difference between *ketiva* and *ḥakika*, between the kind of letter that is inscribed on the parchment of the Torah and the kind that is engraved upon the stone tablets? It lies in the fact that, as Rabbi Shneur Zalman tells us, in *ketiva*, no matter how closely attached the letters are to the parchment, they nevertheless remain two separate entities: letters and parchment. They may be close to each other, well-nigh ineradicable, but ultimately they remain distinct and apart. With *ḥakika*, however, the letters are not at all separate from the stone – the letters and the tablets are organically united, they are one and the same substance. One cannot distinguish between the writing and the stone – they are identical. *Ketiva* keeps the message separate from the scroll upon which it is inscribed, while *ḥakika* has them inextricably bound up as one substance.

There is little doubt which is more significant. It is *ḥakika*. Rabbi Shneur Zalman analogizes these two types of writing to the two categories of spiritual development. The lower one is that of *omeid*, which characterizes one who has attained a certain spiritual station, no matter how high, but it is stationery, standing – there is no motion upward or onwards. The greater level is that of *halikha*, going – the ability to progress and grow and develop. Inscription leads to the stationery spiritual status of *omeid*, whereas engraving inspires the spiritual progressiveness called *halikha*.

Thus we can understand the first several words of this morning's *sidra*: "If you will go in my statutes" (Leviticus 26:3). The word for statutes or laws is here rendered as "*ḥukot*." Normally, we interpret this particular word for laws as referring to those commandments for which man cannot discover any rational explanation. However, according to the interpretation of Rabbi Shneur Zalman, these here refer to those laws which must become part and parcel of the human personality – they must yield the quality of *ḥakika*. What the Torah means to tell us, therefore, is "*im beḥukotai teleikhu*" – if you will observe the Torah in such a manner that it will be for you a *ḥakika*, organically bound up with your own soul and heart and mind, integrated into your personality – then you will achieve the ability to "walk," the superb spiritual attainment of *halikha*.

Now this is a powerful idea and crucial insight. There are, essentially, two approaches to Judaism, two orientations towards our tradition. According to the first, it is possible to accept one's Judaism as a kind of additive to the rest of one's life. It is like the vitamin D that is added to the milk – the same vitamin could well be added to any other substance and enrich it, without changing and transforming that substance. So, some people take their Judaism only as a kind of medicine or vitamin, but it is not part and parcel of their lives. Here, Judaism has been reduced to a religion like all other religions. Just as a Methodist might consider himself a human being, a son, a husband, a father, an American, a professional, who happens to be a Methodist or worship in the Methodist fashion, so the Jew is an American like all other Americans, a human being like all other human beings, no different essentially, just that he happens to have a Jewish religion. He and his Judaism remain two separate and distinct entities. This is the way of *ketiva*. In this case, one's Judaism is like ink written upon parchment – there is a message, it can be read, but the message and the person remain apart from each other.

The greater way is the second, the Judaism of *hakika*. Here the message of Judaism is deeply engraved upon the tablets of one's heart. One's Torah and one's self are organically united – they are integrated with each other.

The first way, that of *ketiva*, is spiritually superficial, whereas the way of *hakika* is religiously profound. The way of *ketiva* is ceremonial and ritual. One leads to a "normal" life and adds thereto a number of interesting observances. The second way, however, that of *hakika*, is indeed a "way of life" – "*im behukotai teleikhu*," "if you will walk in my statutes." The way of *hakika* leads to *halikha*, to going, to a "way," to progress, to growth. The first way is such that it cannot stand up in times of crisis, and to such a person Judaism is regarded as excess baggage in times of tension. The way of "engraving," however, is the kind that lasts forever and, like letters etched in stone, can weather all kinds of storms and inclement circumstances. The way of *hakika* is not merely a matter of dramatic or sentimental rituals – it is the kind of "way" by which a man refers to Torah to deal with the most real and basic and crucial problems of his life.

This same difference between Torah as superadded and Torah as organically united with the individual is seen by our Rabbis (Zohar, *Pinḥas* 232) as accounting for the distinction between Moses and all the other prophets. The other prophets received a message of God from without. They heard a voice or saw a vision and the voice and the vision came from above, from outside of themselves. They were holy, sacred, noble individuals who acted on the basis of this divine message; but the Presence was like ink on parchment – separate from the individuality of the prophet. With Moses, however, the Rabbis told us, it was as if the Divine Presence spoke forth from within Moses, from his very throat! It was a not a revelation that came to him from without himself – it was a revelation that issued from within himself. Moses' personality dissolved in the presence of God. His identity was absorbed in that of God. He was organically bound up with the message of the Lord and integrated with the *Shekhina*.

In a measure, this *ḥakika* must apply to all Jews. An English gentile, a distinguished historian, Professor MacMurray once put it this way: "Whereas other people have a religion, the Jews are the only people who are religious." What he meant, of course, is that for others, religion is expressed exclusively in terms of *ketiva*, whereas Jews seek to attain *ḥakika*. Unfortunately, however, this applies only to the full and complete Jew – and such a person is in a minority. With most of us, regretfully, this is not completely true. Too often our Judaism is just an added element to a life that otherwise is untouched by its sanctity. For too many of us it is unfortunately true that our Judaism could easily be peeled off, like old ink off yellowed parchment.

The differences between *ketiva* and *ḥakika*, between an allegiance that remains external to a person and the kind of commitment that catches a person up in a burning oneness with his ideals, are serious and of the greatest significance. There are clear ways of telling them apart.

For one thing, a *ketiva* relation to Judaism generally does not last too long. In times of tension and stress, the letters are chipped off the parchment – the Jew loses his Judaism, the message becomes garbled, the letters do not make too much sense, the sentences and the verses do not read in the old cadences. When, however, there is a profound sense of identification with one's tradition and faith, and the word of God is inscribed in one's very heart, then it remains permanent, unexchangeable, and indelible. Then, no matter what the vicissitudes that life brings, one's Jewishness remains unimpaired.

Furthermore, as we indicated, a *ketiva* relationship to Judaism means that one is an *omeid* – one remains stationary and cannot make progress in one's religious life. If, however, one practices a *hakika* type of Judaism, such an individual will constantly grow and develop, and will partake of a life of *Halakha* which leads to spiritual *halikha*, progress and growth.

Moreover, every person must have some kind of commitment with which he can truly identify. Unless one is to live his life totally "alienated," completely without rhyme or reason, lost in the limbo of vacuity, one must have something with which one can feel organically bound up. If the sense of *hakika* will not be to Torah and Judaism and the tradition, it must be with something quite different. What a remarkable coincidence that this morning's *haftara* tells us about the other side of that coin. In the first verse of the seventeenth chapter of Jeremiah we read the brooding words of the prophet who tells us that "The sin of Judah is written with a pen of iron and with a point of diamond; *harusha al luah libam*, it is engraved upon the tablets of their heart!" Here is a stark contrast: Either it will be "*im behukotai teleikhu*," the sense of loyalty to God's ways will be engraved upon the tablets of our lives; or else it will be "the sin of Judah," Jewish failure, Jewish bankruptcy, spiritual disaster, which will become "*harusha al luah libam*," engraved upon the tablets of our hearts! We cannot expect long to remain in that never-never land where the tablets of the heart remain untouched. In the end, some message and meaning must be inscribed "with a pen of iron and with a point of a diamond." Which shall it be – the *hakika* of God's ways and statutes, of Jewish pride and loyalty, or the *harusha* of "the sin of Judah," of Jewish disloyalty and backsliding?

The most important test as to whether a person's Judaism is accepted and lived by that individual in a sense of *ketiva* or *hakika* is the immediacy with which that person identifies himself. Wake a person in the middle of the night and ask him, "Who are you?" and demand an immediate answer – and you will know how that person regards himself, what his sense of identity is. If that person says, "a man," or "a stockbroker," or "a Republican," or "a husband," or any one of such answers, you will know the essence of that person's self-definition. What we must strive for is to become so organically at one with our Jewishness that our immediate answer will be: "I am a Jew!"

The Torah already told us of this phenomenon concerning the mysterious figure of Jonah, that ancient prophet who fled from God and "rocked the boat." He was aboard ship when, because of him, God caused a storm to brew at sea and to threaten the passengers with disaster. When they realized that all this was the fault of Jonah, who had kept apart from the others and was unknown to them, they approached him and said to him: "What do you do and where do you come from? What is your country and where do you hail from?" In other words: "Who are you?" And without premeditation, the response came immediately from the old prophet aboard that storm-tossed ship in the eye of the tempest: "I am a Hebrew and I worship the Lord God of Heaven!" (Jonah 1:9) That is how Jonah saw himself and identified himself: "I am a Jew!"

It is precisely this which we must seek to foster within ourselves and families. Our Judaism must be so engraved in our personalities that we should immediately identify ourselves as Jews who worship God, as children of Torah, as members of the covenant community of Israel! The Torah that is written into our souls is not that of *ketiva* but that of *ḥakika*, not merely that of a scroll of the Torah, but that of the tablets of the Law!

This indeed spells the difference between day school education and other forms of Jewish instruction. The difference is not only in the number of hours that we try to give our children training in Jewish law and life. It is the question primarily of whether their Jewishness will be *ketiva*, merely superadded to an otherwise rich curriculum, or *ḥakika*, part and parcel of their lives, their hopes, their aspirations. This is the problem of integration for Jewish education: Can we successfully integrate the sense of Judaism and Jewishness into the personalities of our students?

This indeed, is what should distinguish Orthodoxy from all other kinds of Judaism. Orthodoxy is not merely a matter of more observance. It is not only a question of conscious piety.

One cannot set up a straight yardstick as the criterion of Judaism and say that if one observes only so much he is Reform, if a bit more he is Conservative, and as one goes higher up the measuring rod of observance, one turns Orthodox. By no means! Orthodoxy or Torah Judaism means *hakika* Judaism. It means that no matter what the degree of his success or failure in his observance, one must identify as a loyal Jew; one must feel at one with one's Torah, with one's God, with one's people. An Orthodox Jew is one in whom the Torah is engraved upon the tablets of his heart – who bears the Torah upon the tablets within.

On this Sabbath before Shavuot, when we celebrate the giving of the Torah at Sinai, that lesson must be repeated and relearned. We must strive to reaccept not only a written Law, but an engraved Law.

The famed Hasidic teacher, a younger contemporary of the Ba'al Shem Tov, Rabbi Pinhas of Koretz, once said the following: Hasidism teaches that there is a spark of Godliness in every human being. God dwells within us. But the Zohar also teaches that God and Torah are mystically identical – therefore, it must be equally true that there is a spark of Torah within each Jewish soul, that Torah dwells in every Jew. Hence, Shavuot means something very special and different from what we usually believe. The first revelation at Mount Sinai is one at which God gave the Torah from without – we stood below at the foot of the mountain, and God gave the Torah "from Heaven," from above. But since then we have the Torah within ourselves. Therefore, at Shavuot time, it now becomes our sacred duty and obligation to reveal the Torah to ourselves from within ourselves! We must express the latent Torah that lies within each of us and strives for self-expression.

In a word, we must be inspired to a *hakika* type of Judaism where we shall forever remain bound up with our faith, our leaning, our tradition, our Law. As we enter the season of the giving of the Torah, may we achieve this lofty goal; and may we thereby achieve the level of *halikha*, of "going" – from strength to strength, from love to love, from greatness to greatness.

In This Hour of Crisis[1]

This is an hour of crisis, not only for Israel as a state but for Israel as a people. Our destiny and the destiny of our children and children's children after us is being forged by the soldiers of Israel on lonely outposts in the Gaza strip and on the heights overlooking the Gulf of Aqaba. No Jew can afford to look upon the tense situation as an outsider. As Mordecai the Jew said to Queen Esther, highly placed in non-Jewish society and politics, "Do not imagine that you will escape in the king's house" (Esther 4:13) – do not imagine that you will find safety while danger befalls the rest of the House of Israel.

The Arab guns aimed at the heart of Israel are aimed at our hearts. The stranglehold on the Gulf of Aqaba, the lifeline of the *medina* (nation), is a stranglehold on our throats. And the Russian contempt for the State of Israel bespeaks the old, traditional Russian contempt for all of us as Jews.

---

1. May 27, 1967. The sermon was delivered approximately a week before the breakout of the Six Day War.

How ought we to react in this grave hour? How have Jews always and should Jews now react?

The archetypical and symbolic confrontation between Israel and its enemies was that between Jacob and Esau. When Jacob, surrounded by his wives and children and his retinue, heard that the armed columns of Esau were marching towards him with vengeance in their hearts, Rashi (Genesis 32:9) tells us that he prepared a threefold strategy – he prepared himself for prayer, for gifts, and for war. It is this threefold approach that must become the pattern for our attitude as well.

The gift that Jacob presented to his brother was a form of legitimate appeasement of a bloodthirsty aggressor, in an attempt to turn his hatred into good will. Indeed, it happened to work for Jacob. But it cannot work for Israel today. First, you cannot placate an enemy who is implacable. Those of us who saw King Faisal on television two days ago heard him declare his avowed intention of exterminating Israel, and President Nasser said the same thing yesterday. Nothing less than that would satisfy our enemies. Moreover, Israel has nothing left to give. It has given all but the bare skeletal structure necessary for the survival of a modern country.

Hence, our gift must be the gift that we American Jews are going to give to the Jews and the government of the State of Israel – in other words, our accelerated participation in that great and historic venture known as the UJA. No Jew who fails to give, and to significantly increase his pledge over the past, has a moral right to be proud that he is a Jew. This year Israel faces unusual economic difficulty – the present fall-off in tourism, together with the stupendous military expenditures that it must undertake, make the situation and the need grave indeed. Those who will therefore give this year far in excess of what they gave in the past, and far in excess of what they are able to give, will be performing an invaluable service. Those who do not do so are, with all their talk, valueless for Israel. Their talk, their worry, their advice, their concern, their pride, their keeping their ears glued to the radio – all this is meaningless!

The Jewish Center family will have an opportunity on June 7th to demonstrate the extent of its commitment. I should like to see an enthusiastic response like never before. It behooves us to give our gift before we are solicited, and to prepare a gift that will tell Israel that we have not faltered, and tell all the world that Israel does not stand alone.

The second part of that strategy is war. Can we participate in war if it should be necessary?

Yes we can, and yes it is necessary. There are many ways to fight a war, many fronts, and many weapons. Our contribution, though not military, must not be under-estimated.

For one thing, we must undertake an indefatigable political campaign. As members of a subculture in this great democracy, it is entirely proper that we make our opinion felt where such opinions carry weight. We must undertake to inform the President of the United States, by letter and telegram, that we support his support of Israel, and to tell him as well as our senators and representatives that it was at the urging of an American Secretary of State that Israel gave up much of its precious victory in Sinai, and that the United States has treaty obligations to Israel. This is one campaign in which we can participate immediately after the Sabbath is over.

Another way of making our political influence felt, in a more social manner, will come tomorrow morning when we shall participate physically in demonstrating our support for the State of Israel. We must all take our families and be present at the "Salute to Israel Parade."

Even more directly, our young people can volunteer to help in Israel. Let them be encouraged. American law forbids military service on behalf of a foreign power. But there is much urgent work to be done in place of Israel's men and women who have been pressed into military service. People are urgently needed, and young people should by all means participate in the "Summer Work in Israel" program which has now been expanded, and in the "*Sheirut La'am*" which offers one or two years of service in Israel. The medical services and all other specialties are urgently needed – but Israel even needs people just to dig trenches and build shelters.

So far, it is good to report that results have been most encouraging. Let no one henceforth speak flippantly of "the vanishing Jews of America!" The volunteer offers have been extremely heartening. I am told that only yesterday a surgeon called from San Francisco to New York to offer his services, provided that his two sons would be taken with him. Of particular interest to this congregation is the fact that a brief notice pinned on the bulletin board at Yeshiva University produced, in thirty-six hours, more than three hundred volunteers! I myself have been on the phone with a number of students, including a number of young ladies from Yavneh, who have asked my intercession with their families to permit them to go forthwith to Israel. There is something ineffably precious about the Jewish soul which allows it to express its idealism so immediately and so openly. Each in his or her own way, therefore, can participate in this great war.

We are an irenic, peace-loving people. Our hopes and prayers are for peace not only for us but for the entire world. The author of the *Or HaHayyim* has made this comment in a beautiful interpretation of a verse in today's *sidra*. We read, "And ye shall dwell securely in your land (*be'artzekhem*)" (Leviticus 26:5), followed by "And I shall give peace to the land (*ba'aretz*)" (Leviticus 26:6). But, asks the *Or HaHayyim*, if we were already told that God will let us dwell securely in our land, surely that includes peace – why then repeat the promise that God will give peace to the land? In his answer he distinguishes between "*artzekhem*" and "*eretz*": The first verse refers to security in "*artzekhem*," "your land," which means the Land of Israel. The second verse, however, refers to the granting of peace in "*eretz*," which should be translated not as "the land," but "the world!" In addition to our own national security, we are committed to the great hope and striving for peace throughout the world.

However, when duty and destiny call upon us to work so that others might bear arms on behalf of Israel, or even, if need be, that we do so ourselves, we shall not be found hesitating or faltering! If we were a nation like other nations, this fight would still be noble, but natural. Our existence is at stake, and we shall not submit to the murderous ambitions of that Hitler of the Nile, to those hysterical pygmies of Damascus, or to that venal and obnoxious monarch of the desert kingdom of slave traders.

But Israel is more than that. The creation of the State of Israel was the minimum act by the powers of the world by which they salvaged the barest trace of human dignity left to them. Israel is a state conceived in the ghettos of Europe, born in the death camps of Auschwitz and

Treblinka, delivered in the detention camps of Cyprus, and swaddled in the rags by which the Western powers blindfolded themselves to our agony and stuffed their ears not to hear our cry of anguish.

Israel is a penance paid by Russia for Babi Yar,[2] by England for the Struma,[3] by the United States for its refusal to hear the cry of the refugees in time, by the Catholic countries for the silence of the Deputy Pope, by each and every country for its own public and private crimes against the people of the Lord.

When we shall, therefore, act in defense of Israel, we will be fighting not only for Israel's and our existence, but in effect for the honor of Russia and England and America and France and all of mankind, whether they know it or not, realize or not, care or not, appreciate it or not, even whether they want it or not. For we shall ever remain, as Yehuda haLevi has called us, the heart of the nations and their conscience.

"The sword and the Book were given wrapped together from Heaven" (Leviticus Rabba, *Behukotai* 35:6). We have given the world its Book, and now the People of the Book fight with a sword of courage and honor. For that charge and that mission are decreed from Heaven!

Finally, the third element in this Jewish strategy first taught by Jacob is *tefilla*, prayer. We can perform that by keeping the present situation in mind every time we speak in our *tefillot* of Jerusalem and Zion. In addition, we shall at the conclusion of services today recite special prayers for the welfare of the State of Israel.

But wedded to prayer is the concept of hope. Our prayer and our outlook must always be hopeful, never desperate.

I would like to commend to your attention an insight which speaks not only of hope but offers a perspective that goes far beyond the parochial limits of power politics. Our *sidra*, in enumerating the blessings God promises us, says: "And I shall turn to you," "And I shall

---

2. A massacre at Babi Yar, from September 29-30th, 1941, claimed the lives of 33,000 Jews.
3. The ss Struma was a ship chartered to carry Jewish refugees from Romania to British-controlled Palestine during WWII. Negotiations between the British and Turkey prevented the ship from entering Palestine, and it was sunk by a Soviet submarine, killing over 700 people on board.

increase you, and make you fruitful," "And I shall keep My covenant with you" (Leviticus 26:9).

On the words "I shall turn to you," Rashi quotes the Sages, who commented (*Torat Kohanim* 2:5): "I shall turn away from all My other preoccupations in order to grant you your reward."

What a strange remark! Are we really to take that so anthropomorphically, so primitively? Is God "busy" with other matters so that He has to take "time off" in order to pay loving attention to us?

An answer is provided to us by Rabbi Mordechai Rogov of Chicago, in his work *Ateret Mordekhai*. He points to the midrash (Genesis Rabba, *Vayeshev* 85:1) which cites the verse, "For I know the thoughts of all men" (Jeremiah 29:11). Applying that verse to the story of Joseph and his brothers, the midrash tells us that the brothers were preoccupied with the selling of Joseph, Joseph was busy bemoaning his own bitter fate, Judah was involved in looking for a wife – but all this while, God was preoccupied with the light of the Messiah! Each of the actors in the great drama thought that he knew the whole story. The brothers saw this as an act of vengeance, Joseph as a bitter tragedy that had reached its nadir, Judah was altogether distracted by an extraneous matter. None of them really saw the entire episode in its true, ultimate perspective. None of them realized that God was not "busy" moving affairs as he individually saw it, but that the Almighty was simply making preparations for the ultimate development of Jewish history, leading to the final redemption. The Joseph story, even more than others, reveals how human intention and divine design can sometimes be utterly different and yet mesh with each other, and how the divine plan often uses humans who do not even appreciate the role that they play.

Mankind, by virtue of its natural human limitations, can see only a segment of reality and experience. But if a person is wise, such an individual recognizes this, and understands that beyond one's own comprehension there is a God whose own designs defy our pitiful human attempts at probing His mysteries. We are all actors who play significant roles in a great drama, but few of us ever have any inkling of the extent and direction of the plot.

So it is with the current episode. Today the Arabs are thinking of a quick victory. Russia sees the entire incident as a chance to dislodge the United States from Vietnam. Israel views it as one great crisis that must be overcome. The United States considers it as an added complication forcing it to juggle both Near-Eastern and Far-Eastern commitments. The United Nations regards it as a need to make up for U Thant's blunder,[4] the biggest in the history of diplomacy.

But our hope and our confidence is that God will take "time out" from the individual considerations of the protagonists of the drama and ultimately reveal to us His true preoccupation: "God was preoccupied with the light of the Messiah," that Almighty God is weaving all these political and military strands into the garment of light that the Messiah will wear, into the intricate designs by which there will come to Israel and all the world the complete redemption.

May, indeed, all our heartache and anxiety, all our worry and preparation for war, be transcended by the great victory and salvation which will come, speedily in our day. And may peace arrive for Israel and all mankind.

---

4. The secretary-general of the UN agreed to pull UN troops out of the Sinai in 1967 in response to a request from Gamal Abdel Nasser, the Egyptian president.

About the Author

R abbi Norman Lamm, former President and Chancellor
of Yeshiva University and Rosh haYeshiva of its affiliated Rabbi Isaac
Elchanan Theological Seminary, is one of the most gifted and profound
Jewish thinkers today. He was the founding editor of *Tradition*, the
journal of Orthodox thought published by the Rabbinical Council of
America, and to this day convenes the Orthodox Forum, a think tank
of rabbis, academicians, and community leaders that meets annually to
discuss topics of concern in the Orthodox community. Before assuming the presidency of Yeshiva University, Rabbi Lamm served for many
years as Rabbi of The Jewish Center, one of New York City's most
prominent and vibrant Orthodox synagogues.

A prolific author in the field of Jewish philosophy and law, a distinguished academician, and a charismatic pulpit rabbi, Rabbi Lamm
has made, and continues to make, an extraordinary impact on the Jewish community. With a rare combination of penetrating scholarship
and eloquence of expression, he presents a view of contemporary Jewish life that speaks movingly to all.

About the Editor

Stuart W. Halpern serves as an Academic Advisor on the Wilf Campus at Yeshiva University, the Assistant Director of the Zahava and Moshael Straus Center for Torah and Western Thought at Yeshiva University, and the Assistant Director of Student Programming and Community Outreach of the Bernard Revel Graduate School of Jewish Studies. He received his BA from the University of Pennsylvania, an MA in Psychology in Education from Teachers College at Columbia University, an MA in Bible from Revel, and his doctorate from the Azrieli Graduate School of Jewish Education and Administration. He is the co-editor of the *Mitokh Ha-Ohel* series and serves on the Steering Committee of the Orthodox Forum.

The fonts used in this book are from the Arno family

Other works by Norman Lamm:

Rav Kook: Man of Faith and Vision (1965)

A Hedge of Roses: Jewish Insights into Marriage and Married Life (1966)

The Royal Reach: Discourses on the Jewish Tradition and the World Today (1970)

Faith and Doubt: Studies in Traditional Jewish Thought (1971:1986:2006)

Torah Lishmah: Torah for Torah's Sake in the Works of Rabbi Hayyim of Volozhin and his Contemporaries (Hebrew 1972, English 1989)

The Good Society: Jewish Ethics in Action (1974)

Torah Umadda: The Encounter of Religious Learning and Worldly Knowledge in the Jewish Tradition (1990:2010)

Halakhot Ve'Halikhot (Hebrew): *Jewish Law and the Legacy of Judaism: Essays and Inquiries in Jewish Law* (1990)

The Shema: Spirituality and Law in Judaism (1998)

The Religious Thought of Hasidism: Text and Commentary (1999)

Seventy Faces (two volumes): *Articles of Faith* (2001)

The Royal Table: A Passover Haggadah (2010)

Festivals of Faith: Reflections on the Jewish Holidays (2011)

The Megillah: Majesty and Mystery (2012)

Derashot LeDorot: A Commentary for the Ages: Genesis (2012)

Derashot LeDorot: A Commentary for the Ages: Leviticus (2013)

Maggid Books
The best of contemporary Jewish thought from
Koren Publishers Jerusalem Ltd.